In case of loss, please return to:

_____

_____

_____

_____

As a reward: $_____

EXPERIENCING GOD

GOD'S INVITATION TO YOUNG ADULTS

RICHARD BLACKABY
HENRY BLACKABY

LifeWay Press®
Nashville, Tennessee

© 2013 LifeWay Press® · Reprinted October 2018

Originally published as *God's Invitation: A Challenge to College Students*

No part of this work may be reproduced or transmitted in any form or by any means, electronic or mechanical, including photocopying and recording, or by any information storage or retrieval system, except as may be expressly permitted in writing by the publisher. Requests for permission should be addressed in writing to LifeWay Press®; One LifeWay Plaza; Nashville, TN 37234.

ISBN 978-1-4300-2864-2 · Item 005601368

Dewey decimal classification: 248.84
Subject headings: ADULTS \ CHRISTIAN LIFE \ GOD—WILL

Cover design by Lauren Randalls Ervin

Unless indicated otherwise, Scripture quotations are taken from the Holy Bible, NEW INTERNATIONAL VERSION®. Copyright © 1973, 1978, 1984 by Biblica Inc. All rights reserved worldwide. Used by permission. Scripture quotation marked AMP is taken from The Amplified® Bible, copyright © 1954, 1958, 1962, 1964, 1965, 1987 by The Lockman Foundation. Used by permission. (lockman.org)

To order additional copies of this resource, write to LifeWay Resources Customer Service; One LifeWay Plaza; Nashville, TN 37234; fax 615-251-5933; phone toll free 800-458-2772; email orderentry@lifeway.com; order online at LifeWay.com; or visit the LifeWay Christian Store serving you.

Printed in the United States of America

Groups Ministry Publishing · LifeWay Resources
One LifeWay Plaza · Nashville, TN 37234

TABLE OF CONTENTS

HENRY T. BLACKABY is the founder and president emeritus of Blackaby Ministries International (blackaby.net), an organization designed to help people experience God. Born in British Columbia, Dr. Blackaby has devoted his lifetime to ministry. He has served as a music director, education director, and pastor in churches in California and Canada, as well as president of Canadian Baptist Theological College and president of the Canadian Southern Baptist Conference. Dr. Blackaby studied English and history at the University of British Columbia as an undergraduate and earned his BD and ThM from Golden Gate Baptist Theological Seminary. He holds five honorary doctorate degrees.

As a pastor in Canada, Henry sensed that in order to reach the nation for Christ, God would have to call young adults, particularly college students, to Himself and then send them out as pastors, missionaries and church workers across the nation. With this in mind, he founded a Bible college where young adults could study the Scriptures and hear God's call upon their lives. During Henry's time as a pastor, numerous young adults were baptized and many of these felt called into full-time Christian service.

Dr. Blackaby later served at the North American Mission Board of the Southern Baptist Convention. There, he led the office for revival and spiritual awakening. He also served as special assistant to the presidents of the International Mission Board and LifeWay Christian Resources. Although he is now officially retired, Dr. Blackaby continues to speak around the world.

Henry is a popular conference speaker and has written several books, including *Experiencing God: Knowing and Doing the Will of God, Fresh Encounter: God's Pattern for Revival and Spiritual Awakening, Called and Accountable, What the Spirit Is Saying to the Churches,* and *Hearing God's Voice.* He was the general editor of the *Experiencing God Study Bible.*

Henry lives with his wife, Marilynn, in Rex, Georgia. He has five children (Richard, Tom, Melvin, Norman, and Carrie), all of whom are serving in Christian ministry.

RICHARD BLACKABY is the oldest child of Henry and Marilynn and has worked extensively with young adults. He is the president of Blackaby Ministries International. Richard graduated from the University of Saskatchewan, where he served as the president of the Baptist Student Union. During that time Richard met his wife, Lisa Cavanaugh, who also was on the student council. Richard was the vice president and then the president of the state student council of the Northwest Baptist Convention. He has an MDiv and a PhD in church history from Southwestern Baptist Theological Seminary and an honorary doctorate from Dallas Baptist University. Richard and Lisa have three children: Michael, Daniel, and Carrie.

Richard served as a senior pastor at Friendship Baptist Church in Winnipeg, and then as the president of the Canadian Southern Baptist Seminary in Cochrane, Alberta Canada for 13 years. He continues to serve as the seminary's chancellor.

Dr. Blackaby has coauthored the following books with his father, Henry Blackaby: *God's Invitation, CrossSeekers, Experiencing God Day by Day, The Experience, Spiritual Leadership: Moving People on to God's Agenda, Hearing God's Voice,* and *Called to Be God's Leader: Lessons from the Life of Joshua.* He has also written *The Seasons of God, The Inspired Leader, Unlimiting God, Putting a Face on Grace,* and *Experiencing God at Home.*

Richard travels internationally speaking on spiritual leadership in the home, church, and marketplace, as well as on spiritual awakening, experiencing God, and the Christian life. Richard regularly ministers to Christian CEOs and business leaders.

AS A YOUNG ADULT, you're at a most important and vulnerable time in your life. A serious Christian will want to prepare and become equipped for God's best. Life is so precious. How you use the life God has given you is critical. Strive to invest your life in such a way that you will have no regrets and will know that your life has been well spent.

You may be in an environment where others influence and pressure you to conform to their values, goals, and lifestyles. This can lead you to lose it all. But remember, as a Christian, you'll always have the presence of the Holy Spirit in your life, exerting a significant influence to go His way which always leads to abundant life. Jesus warned people to:

> "Enter through the narrow gate. For wide is the gate and broad
> is the road that leads to destruction, and many enter through it.
> But small is the gate and narrow the road that leads to life, and
> only a few find it" (Matthew 7:13-14).

We're confident that you truly want life, not destruction. This study is designed to help you experience God—that is to know in your life His ways, His promises, His presence, and His abundant life. Read the Scriptures carefully for "they are your very life" (John 6:63; Deuteronomy 30:11-20). Study with others who also are wanting to experience God. Choose to be accountable to one or more persons who will confront you when they see you making wrong choices which lead you away from God's best. Spend time early, and throughout the day, to "seek the LORD your God ... with all your heart" (Deuteronomy 4:29).

GOD WILL GUIDE YOU DAILY AS YOU GO THROUGH THIS STUDY AND EARNESTLY SEEK HIS WILL.

Remember, God already has wonderful plans for you, "to give you a hope and a future" (Jeremiah 29:11). God will guide you daily as you go through this study and earnestly seek His will.

Throughout this material we have sought to clearly describe how you can experience the joy of knowing and walking with God. We have appreciated our wives, Marilynn and Lisa, as they have been so supportive of our ministries to young adults throughout the years.

ABOUT THIS STUDY

THE PURPOSE OF THIS STUDY is to help you know what God is saying to you and to give practical help as you seek God's will for important decisions such as choosing your career and marriage partner. Our aim is to help you be prepared for the life decisions you will face. This is a Bible study, so keep your Bible handy and look up each verse as directed. Our advice cannot change your life, but God's Word can.

OUR AIM IS TO HELP YOU BE PREPARED FOR THE LIFE DECISIONS YOU WILL FACE.

There are seven sessions that can be covered in seven weeks, one session per week. There are five lessons in each session. It's best to allow time to contemplate the truths you encounter. This study involves much more than the completion of assignments or the reading of a book: Its purpose is for you to encounter God. That will not happen if you rush through the materials, neglect to read all the Scriptures, or cram the hour before your group meets.

There is a weekly Scripture-memory verse that will help you remember the key truths of each chapter. We encourage you to memorize these Scriptures as you go throughout the study.

At the end of each week you will meet with your group to discuss the materials you've studied and to share what God said to you. A group leader should be available to facilitate discussion. His or her role is not to lecture or impart new materials but to lead people to discuss what they have learned that week and what they have committed themselves to do in response.

At the end of each lesson you'll be asked, "What did God say to you during your study today?" and "What are you going to do as a result?" Use the allotted space as well as the margins in your book to keep a journal of what you're hearing God say. Once you've completed the study, you may want to go back and review all God revealed to you.

1

SEEING LIFE FROM GOD'S PERSPECTIVE

> "The LORD Almighty has purposed, and who can thwart him? His hand
> is stretched out, and who can turn it back?" (Isaiah 14:27).

AS GEORGE BERNARD SHAW, the great English playwright, neared the end of his illustrious career, a young man approached him with an intriguing question. He asked, "If you could live your life over and could be any person you have ever known or could be any person in history, who would you want to be?" This was a provocative question, for Shaw had known some of history's greatest men and had been a friend of Winston Churchill. He replied, "I would be the man George Bernard Shaw could have been, but never was." How tragic to come to the end of your life and realize that you never reached your full potential.

In contrast, we recently spent an inspiring evening in the home of an elderly Christian couple. The husband had been diagnosed with terminal, inoperable cancer; his life would end just one month later. As we sat with them in their living room, he reminisced with joy about how God had led him into politics for more than 40 years of civil service. He talked about his Christian radio ministry and all the Christian leaders he had befriended. He and his wife rejoiced that their only son, a believer, also had entered politics and now was a prominent national figure. With great delight they told us that each of their five grandchildren loved God and were seeking to serve Him. Here was a godly man satisfied with his life and ready to die.

Some people face death grudgingly, resentfully, even fearfully. Others approach it with a sense of peace, satisfaction, and triumph. It is our hope that you will live your life in such a way that when the end is near, you will have the assurance of a life well spent. This will happen only if you link your life to God's eternal purposes.

GOD SEES FROM AN ETERNAL VIEW

> "I make known the end from the beginning, from ancient times, what
> is still to come. I say: My purpose will stand, and I will do all that I please.
> … What I have said, that I will bring about; what I have planned, that will
> I do" (Isaiah 46:10-11).

William Borden was born into a wealthy Chicago family in 1887. He had the best this world had to offer: education, world travels, and every physical comfort. By the age of 21 he was a millionaire. Yet Borden's heart was sensitive to God's will for his life. When he was 7, he gave his life to Christ, but it was as a 16-year-old that God began to speak to him very specifically.

During an around-the-world cruise, he met missionaries going to their fields of service. Writing to his mother at the time, he commented: "Your request that I pray to God for His very best plan for my life is not a hard thing to do, for I have been praying that very thing for a long time. … When I look ahead a few years it seems as though the only thing to do is to prepare for the foreign field."

Borden attended Princeton University with the intention of devoting his life to foreign missions. Despite the fact that he loved automobiles, he told his friends that he could not "afford" to purchase one. In reality, every time he considered buying a car, he was overwhelmed with the needs of foreign missions and sent money to those causes instead. It's estimated that during his three years in seminary he gave away more than $70,000!

In December 1912, his education completed, Borden sailed to Cairo, Egypt, for language training before entering mission service in China. While there, Borden contracted cerebral meningitis and died, never having reached his destination. Upon his deathbed, at age 25, he reiterated his life's theme: "No reserve, no retreat, no regrets." In his will he left almost one million dollars to Christian causes.

When news arrived in America that this young millionaire had willingly abandoned his fortune and died in squalid conditions in Egypt, it had an electrifying effect on young adults throughout North America and Europe. Many responded to God's call to missions because of Borden's life, tragically cut short.[1]

Do you consider Borden's life a success? Why or why not?

Could you make the same sacrifices Borden did if you sensed God's leading? Why or why not?

What do you think motivated William Borden?

God did not create you for time but for eternity. Every word, act, and purpose of God is in the context of His eternal perspective. God never acts for the moment but works with the full knowledge of all that has occurred throughout history leading up to the present time. He does not speak or act in your life without knowing what the consequences will be throughout the remainder of human history and eternity. From a human perspective, William Borden's life may have been tragically wasted. From God's eternal perspective, Borden's life was wisely spent.

GOD KNOWS YOUR PAST

Notice God's eternal perspective on your life. Read Ephesians 1:4-6 and Jeremiah 1:5. Reflect on these passages before answering the following two questions.

According to these passages, at what point did God begin preparing for your life?

How could God use your past as He guides your life today?

When God relates to you, He knows everything about you. He's aware of even the smallest details concerning your ancestors and every gene that they've passed down to you. He understands where your shyness came from as well as your intelligence. He knows the origin of every physical weakness and strength. He not only knows what you're like, He knows what has caused you to be who you are.

GOD KNOWS YOUR FUTURE

God's eternal perspective is not limited to looking at the past. He also sees the future. Read carefully what the Scripture below says about this.

> "Your eyes saw my unformed body. All the days ordained for me were written in your book before one of them came to be" (Psalm 139:16).

> "Come, you who are blessed by my Father; take your inheritance, the kingdom prepared for you since the creation of the world" (Matthew 25:34).

Underline those things listed in the verses above that indicate what God knows about your future.

Check the concerns you have about your future.

❑ Getting married   ❑ Your job/career
❑ Having children   ❑ Your health
❑ Length of your life   ❑ Your success in business
❑ Owning your own home   ❑ Health of your parents
❑ Crises you will face   ❑ World peace
❑ Time of Christ's return   ❑ Impact you will have on your world

List ways God's knowledge of your future affects the way He leads you.

God knows everything about your future. He foresees what crises you'll face as well as every triumph you'll enjoy. Because God knows your future, He is able to guide you perfectly day by day. He knows whether it's best for you to be married, to have children, or to remain single. Only God has perfect hindsight as well as foresight and so only He can guide you flawlessly. Just as Jesus confronted His followers, so He challenges you today. He knows what there is around you that has eternal significance and what will pass away before the year ends.

List two ways you currently are investing in eternity.

1.

2.

GOD SPEAKS TO YOU BY THE HOLY SPIRIT

Have you ever thought: It would be easy to live the Christian life if I could just see Jesus and hear Him speaking to me? Perhaps the Christian life might be easier in some ways, but you would not be as compelled to live your life by faith. As the writer of Hebrews pointed out: "Without faith it is impossible to please God" (11:6). Jesus promised His followers He would not abandon them; the heavenly Father would send the Holy Spirit, who would relate to the disciples in exactly the same way Jesus had.

Read the verses below and notice what the Holy Spirit does in your life.

> **"He will give you another Counselor to be with you forever—the Spirit of truth" (John 14:16-17).**

> **"When he comes, he will convict the world of guilt in regard to sin and righteousness and judgment. But when he, the Spirit of truth, comes, he will guide you into all truth. ... He will tell you what is yet to come" (John 16:8,13).**

"The Spirit searches all things, even the deep things of God. For who among men knows the thoughts of a man except the man's spirit within him? In the same way no one knows the thoughts of God except the Spirit of God" (1 Corinthians 2:10-11).

Go back and underline the names given to the Holy Spirit which describe His activity in your life.

What will the Holy Spirit do in your life?

It's the role of the Holy Spirit to lead and teach you in the same way that Jesus related to His disciples. Whether it's knowing what your major in college should be, whom to marry, or what job to pursue, the Holy Spirit will guide you. It is imperative, therefore, that you cultivate your personal relationship with the Spirit of God so you can clearly hear His voice.

What did God say to you during your study today?

What will you do as a result?

GOD EXTENDS AN INVITATION

> " Call to me and I will answer you and tell you great and unsearchable things you do not know" (Jeremiah 33:3).

Henry has been a keen observer of current events. He would watch national leaders on television and read about world affairs in the newspaper. Although he prayed for government leaders, he'd never known them personally. Then one day I received an invitation to visit the president of the United States in the Oval Office. When he discussed issues of concern with the president, he knew he was speaking with someone who actually had the power to make a difference.

Had Henry lobbied and campaigned to gain the opportunity to speak to the president, he might never have been successful. Instead, he received an invitation, and by that invitation he was given immediate and personal access. This is similar to the Christian experience. We can go through life observing events taking place around us. We can discuss them with our family and friends and yet be oblivious to any way we can make a difference. Suddenly God may reveal His active presence in the midst of these events. The Bible calls this revelation. God shows us something that we couldn't have discovered on our own. The writer of Proverbs observed: "Where there is no revelation, the people cast off restraint" (Proverbs 29:18). This means that without God's revelation, you will have no sense of direction nor will you lead a purposeful life guided toward God's best. Spiritual truth isn't discovered, it's revealed. When God presents truth to you, His revelation is also His invitation to adjust your life to that truth.

When God told Noah a flood was coming, it was something Noah never could have discovered on his own (until it was too late!). But once Noah understood the truth God had revealed, he immediately adjusted his life to God's Word. God's revelation was also an invitation for Noah to adjust his life to God's activity of judgment on the land. Noah didn't have to accept God's invitation, but to reject it would have been disastrous. When God told Moses He was going to rescue the children of Israel from Egypt, His revelation also came with an invitation. Moses had to make a choice. He could no longer herd sheep in the wilderness and remain obedient to the revelation he had received from God. From Genesis to Revelation God speaks to His people, calling, teaching, and guiding them. While you're searching for answers, God will be seeking to guide you into His best for you.

As the Holy Spirit lives in you and guides you, He will use Scriptures to encourage, convict, and lead you to experience the full life that only God can give.

Read the verses below and notice how God uses the Bible to help you understand His will.

> **"Do not let this Book of the Law depart from your mouth; meditate on it day and night, so that you may be careful to do everything written in it. Then you will be prosperous and successful" (Joshua 1:8).**

> **"If you remain in me and my words remain in you, ask whatever you wish, and it will be given you" (John 15:7).**

> **"All Scripture is God-breathed and is useful for teaching, rebuking, correcting and training in righteousness, so that the man of God may be thoroughly equipped for every good work" (2 Timothy 3:16-17).**

List the things God says He will do for you as you obey His Word.

Watch carefully as you read and study God's Word. What the Spirit is teaching is God's will for your life (1 Corinthians 2:9-10). As you read the Bible each day, the Holy Spirit will guide you through verses which reveal God's will.

For example, you may be reading your Bible and come across Matthew 15:4: "God said, 'Honor your father and mother.' "The Holy Spirit may focus your attention on this verse. You try to continue reading, but you cannot leave verse 4. You begin to have the uneasy feeling that God is applying this verse to you. You realize that your parents have done some things that have made you angry and you've held bitterness in your heart. You remember some of the painful words you exchanged the last time you were together. The Holy Spirit affirms that nothing they have done caused them to deserve the lack of respect you demonstrated. You realize that God takes this extremely seriously and so you repent and take action to restore your relationship with your parents. God has just used the Bible to guide you.

What's one thing you've heard God saying to you recently as you read His Word?

How have you acted on it?

GOD SPEAKS TO YOU THROUGH PRAYER

The Holy Spirit will also speak to you during your times of prayer. Prayer is not a one-way conversation where you tell God all your plans and concerns. When you come into the presence of Almighty God, what He says is far more important than what you want to say. God will speak to you in your prayer time if you'll listen. Notice in the Scripture below what God wants to tell you during your prayer times.

> "I say to you: Ask and it will be given to you; seek and you will find; knock and the door will be opened to you. For everyone who asks receives; he who seeks finds; and to him who knocks, the door will be opened" (Luke 11:9-10).

> "In the same way, the Spirit helps us in our weakness. We do not know what we ought to pray for, but the Spirit himself intercedes for us with groans that words cannot express. And he who searches our hearts knows the mind of the Spirit, because the Spirit intercedes for the saints in accordance with God's will" (Romans 8:26-27).

In these verses, underline the things God promises to do when you pray.

What does God show you when you pray?

God does have a will for your life. As you pray, God speaks His will to you. God spoke to Moses on Mount Sinai (Exodus 32:7-14), to Daniel in captivity (Daniel 9), and to Jesus during His earthly ministry (Matthew 17:1-8; 26:36-46). When you pray, alone or with others, be alert to any prompting of the Holy Spirit, for He will be speaking God's will to you.

For example, you may be praying one day when suddenly the Holy Spirit brings to mind a mission project to the homeless that your church is planning to undertake. You didn't sign up to help because you feel uncomfortable around homeless people. You try to return to what you were praying about, but you cannot seem to forget the mission project. Then the Spirit brings to mind Matthew 25:35: "I was hungry and you gave me something to eat, I was thirsty and you gave me something to drink, I was a stranger and you invited me in." The Spirit reminds you that Christ left the comforts of heaven to come and minister to humankind and that Jesus Himself had no place to lay His head. In that moment you know that, despite your fears, you must sign up for the mission project. God, through prayer, has just rearranged your priorities.

What is one thing God has said to you in your prayer times recently?

What are you doing as a result?

GOD SPEAKS TO YOU THROUGH CIRCUMSTANCES
A third way the Holy Spirit speaks to you is through the everyday events of your life. The Holy Spirit was convicting a young man named Kyle about his need to tithe his earnings from his job to his local church. Every cent was precious, but the Spirit persisted. Finally, during a service at his church, Kyle placed $40 in the offering plate. As he was leaving the auditorium, a church member approached him and said God had impressed her to give him a card. At home, Kyle opened the card to find four $10 bills! Through circumstances in this young man's life, God spoke loud and clear!

Read carefully the Scriptures below that describe how God speaks to you through your circumstances.

> "I tell you the truth, the Son can do nothing by himself; he can do only what he sees his Father doing, because whatever the Father does the Son also does. For the Father loves the Son and shows him all he does" (John 5:19-20).

> "Jesus answered, 'I am the way and the truth and the life. No one comes to the Father except through me'" (John 14:6).

> "We know that in all things God works for the good of those who love him, who have been called according to his purpose" (Romans 8:28).

In John 5 how did Jesus determine His Father's will for His life?

Who's the only person, according to John 14:6, who knows the entire "truth" of your circumstances?

How does Romans 8:28 indicate we should look at even our worst circumstances?

Circumstances can be wonderful opportunities for God to speak to you. Jesus said in John 5 that He never did anything on His own initiative. He always observed the events around Him in order to recognize God at work. When He saw God working, Jesus adjusted His life and joined Him. Jesus told His disciples in John 14:6 that He was the "truth." This means that only He can reveal the truth of your circumstances. Romans 8:28 says there will never be a situation in your life where God cannot speak to you and bring something good into your life.

How have you recently heard God speaking to you through your circumstances? In the past?

What have you done as a result?

Often God speaks to you through another Christian. A student minister told us the story of a young lady named Cheryl who visited his office. Cheryl related her financial problems and asked: "Do you think God could help me find a job?" The minister assured her that He could and began to tell of times when God had provided for him. While he spoke, a church member poked her head in the office and said, "Hey, Cheryl, I'm glad I caught you! Listen, when you get finished here I need to see you. A position has opened up where I work and I wanted to recommend you. I need to talk to you about it." Cheryl assured her she would and then turned to the minister and asked in the same desperate voice with which she had begun their conversation: "So, do you really think God could provide me a job?" God will speak to you through the people of God. Be sensitive to His voice when He does!

Notice in the Scriptures below what God says He will do through the local church.

> "In Christ we who are many form one body, and each member belongs to all the others" (Romans 12:5).

> "To each one the manifestation of the Spirit is given for the common good" (1 Corinthians 12:7).

> "It was he who gave some to be apostles, some to be prophets, some to be evangelists, and some to be pastors and teachers, to prepare God's people for works of service, so that the body of Christ may be built up until we all reach unity in the faith and in the knowledge of the Son of God and become mature, attaining to the whole measure of the fullness of Christ" (Ephesians 4:11-13).

Where does God place you when you become a Christian?

Why does the Holy Spirit manifest Himself to you?

How and why does God equip members in the church?

A church is a living body of Christ, and each member helps all the others grow to completeness in Christ (Ephesians 4:7,11-16). When you are an active member in a local church, God will speak clearly to you through the other members of the church family. The Holy Spirit will manifest Himself in your life in order to encourage others in the church toward Christian maturity.

How has God recently spoken to you through your church?

What did God say to you during your study today?

What will you do as a result?

GOD FOLLOWS A PATTERN

> "As Jesus walked beside the Sea of Galilee, he saw Simon and his brother Andrew casting a net into the lake, for they were fishermen. 'Come, follow me,' Jesus said, 'and I will make you fishers of men.' At once they left their nets and followed him. When he had gone a little farther, he saw James son of Zebedee and his brother John in a boat, preparing their nets. Without delay he called them, and they left their father Zebedee in the boat with the hired men and followed him" (Mark 1:16-20).

As a young man, D. L. Moody was well on his way to becoming a successful businessman. He had the natural ability and ambition to go to the top. Then Moody became a Christian and his priorities began to change. One day while Moody was in Britain, he heard Henry Varley declare: "This world has yet to see what God can do with a man fully consecrated to Him." The Holy Spirit used these words to burn deeply into Moody's soul. Speaking to Varley later, Moody confessed: "Those were the words sent to my soul, through you, from the living God. As I crossed the wide Atlantic, the boards of the deck of the vessel were engraved with them, and when I reached Chicago, the very paving stones seemed marked with 'Moody, the world has yet to see what God will do with a man fully consecrated to Him.'"

Moody ultimately responded to God with the prayer, "By God's help I aim to be that man." God was doing more than just issuing a challenge to a young man, for He knew what He could make of Moody and how He could use his life. God, through the challenge of Henry Varley, was inviting Moody to join Him in His activity rather than to continue pursuing his own goals. So mightily did God use Moody, it's estimated that more than 100 million people heard him preach during his ministry; three schools were formed; two Christian publishing houses were begun; and a mission movement that included some of the greatest missionaries in modern history was inspired.

Since Moody's death his writings and influence continue to win millions of people to God. Moody never could have dreamed of all that God wanted to do through his life, yet when he heard Him speak, he responded to the invitation.

THE DISCIPLE JOHN

God will relate to you in a manner that is unique and personal. Throughout Scripture there is a general pattern God used as He invited men and women to join in His eternal activity. John the apostle could serve as a model of this pattern. Notice in Mark 1:16-20 the simplicity of Jesus' invitation.

In John's life there are five realities to guide you as you look to see how God involves you in His work.

1. God is always at work around you.
2. God loves you and invites you to become involved with Him in His work.
3. God speaks to you by His Holy Spirit through the Bible, prayer, circumstances, and the church.
4. God's invitation will create a crisis of belief, requiring you to make adjustments in your life.
5. When you obey, you experience God's power working through you, and you bring Him glory.

1. God is always at work around you. Since the beginning of creation, God had been planning to send a Savior to earth to save His people from their sins. God promised Abraham that through his descendants all the nations of the earth would be blessed (Genesis 22:18). King David also anticipated the Savior's arrival (Psalm 22; 110). Great prophets such as Isaiah spoke of the time of the Messiah's coming (Isaiah 7:14; 9:1-7; 53). And now, during John's lifetime, while the mighty Roman Empire seemed invincible and at a time when the Jewish nation was defeated, God's eternal plan was culminating in the coming of His Son Jesus. As Jesus walked in the region of Galilee, people were unaware of the staggering reality that the Son of God Himself was talking to them face to face. From a human perspective, God's people had been defeated by the dreaded Romans. From God's perspective, His activity continued as He had determined, unhindered by men. From a human perspective, the Roman Empire had created intricate roads, fortresses, armies, and a navy that ensured theirs was the most significant power in the world. From God's perspective the Romans had been unknowing instruments of His plan, preparing a safe and extensive travel network on which missionaries could take His good news around the world.

2. God loves you and invites you to become involved with Him in His work. John was a young man, the son of a fisherman, when he first met Jesus. His father, Zebedee, wanted him to carry on the family business. A religious education had never been considered. John was fortunate, for he was inheriting a business that was apparently successful, considering he had partners as well as servants. Had John spent his life as a fisherman on the tiny Sea of Galilee, he would have died unknown to history.

God loved John and invited him to join in His work (Mark 3:14). John would be a friend who savored Jesus' company and whose fellowship Jesus enjoyed. John was receiving an invitation to walk with the Son of God. It's more significant to be a fisher of men than a fisher of fish! God was unfolding His eternal plan, and John was to have a part in it. Jesus knew all that John's life could become. John knew only that he should respond to Jesus' invitation.

3. God speaks to you by His Holy Spirit through the Bible, prayer, circumstances, and the church. John had the singular opportunity to hear Jesus' voice and to look Him in the face. When Jesus said, "Come, follow Me," John left his career and immediately followed Jesus. When he was sent out to preach in the surrounding villages, John went. When Jesus had special times of prayer with His closest disciples, John participated.

Whenever Jesus spoke, it was an invitation for John to believe God and to obey Him. The time for Jesus to speak to His followers in this manner, however, lasted only a few short years. As Jesus was preparing to leave the disciples in His physical form, He promised John and the other disciples, "The Counselor, the Holy Spirit, whom the Father will send in my name, will teach you all things and will remind you of everything I have said to you" (John 14:26). Although Jesus would no longer relate to John as an earthly man, He would send the Holy Spirit, who would open John's understanding to what the Heavenly Father was saying through the Bible, prayer, circumstances, and the church.

Jesus assured John that whenever he read the Scriptures, the Holy Spirit would "guide you into all truth" (John 16:13). Furthermore, when John prayed, the Holy Spirit would be present to help him understand what God was saying to him. It appears that John was praying when he saw his amazing apocalypse on the Isle of Patmos (Revelation 1:10). John was encouraged that he would never face a situation in his life where the Holy Spirit was not present to help him understand and learn from his circumstances (John 14:18). Finally, John came to understand that it was in the context of the local church that believers could encounter the risen Christ in a profound way (Revelation 3:20).

> THROUGHOUT SCRIPTURE THERE IS A GENERAL
> PATTERN GOD USED AS HE INVITED
> MEN AND WOMEN TO JOIN
> IN HIS ETERNAL ACTIVITY.

4. God's invitation will create a crisis of belief, requiring you to make adjustments in your life. When Jesus invited John to join in His activity, it created a crisis of belief for John. That is, although John believed in God, he now was being asked to do an impossible task. This is the difference between head knowledge and faith in God. John was not trained to be a religious leader or teacher. He was trained to catch fish. Now Jesus was asking him to leave what he knew to do something unfamiliar. John still was a young man and probably not old enough to garner much respect as a teacher or preacher in his community. Furthermore, John's father, Zebedee, would be left behind. We can only speculate whether John, as he followed Jesus, cast a painful look back at his father, still in their boat.

John's character was not conducive to being a church leader. He had a hot temper, which prompted Jesus to nickname him a "Son of Thunder" (Mark 3:17). When a Samaritan village did not welcome Jesus, John and his brother James offered to call down fire from heaven to destroy the inhospitable villagers (Luke 9:54). Not only was John prone to anger, but he was pursuing his personal ambition. John and his brother dared to approach Jesus to ask if they might have the two highest places of honor in Jesus' kingdom (Mark 10:35-41). Being probably the youngest disciple, this showed strong ambition and a willingness to get the better of others to gain personal advantage. These character flaws in John made his becoming a world-changing, church-planting, Scripture-writing apostle an impossible feat in human terms. Fortunately for John, Jesus not only invited him to attempt the impossible but also developed his character until John was the kind of man to whom He would entrust God-sized assignments.

5. When you obey, you experience God's power working through you, and you bring Him glory. Despite John's shaky beginnings, he came to understand that each time he obeyed Christ, God worked through him and received glory. After John received the Holy Spirit, he experienced the incredible joy of being used by God to bring salvation to others. While John and Peter were on their way to the temple, they encountered a man who had been lame all his life. When they healed the man, he experienced salvation. A crowd soon gathered and listened to the Gospel (Acts 3). As a result of their witness, many believed and the church grew to more than 5,000 men (Acts 4:4). Peter and John were used by God so significantly that Acts notes: "When they saw the courage of Peter and John and realized that they were unschooled, ordinary men, they were astonished and they took note that these men had been with Jesus" (Acts 4:13). So filled with the Spirit were John and his companions that "the place where they were meeting was shaken. With great power the apostles continued to testify to the resurrection of the Lord Jesus, and much grace was upon them all" (Acts 4:31,33).

John wrote the Gospel of John, 1–3 John, and the Book of Revelation. These letters would be read, preached, taught, and studied in every language around the world. Surely John could not have imagined that God would choose to use a fisherman to be part of such an enormous work! The more John obeyed, however, the more God involved him in His work, and the greater glory God received through John's life.

List the five realities of God's invitation.

1.

2.

3.

4.

5.

Is God inviting you to become involved with Him in His activity? What is He inviting you to do?

Which reality of God's invitation are you currently experiencing?

How are you responding to God's invitation?

What did God say to you during your study today?

What will you do as a result?

GOD INVITES US TO AN INTIMATE RELATIONSHIP

> "As I was with Moses, so I will be with you; I will never leave you nor forsake you" (Joshua 1:5).

During the time I (Henry) served as pastor, I had the privilege of performing the weddings of many young adults and would counsel with them during the weeks leading up to their wedding. There was always a glow about them as they excitedly prepared for their future together. A couple who came to my home for premarital counseling spoke of the plans they had and the arrangements they were making for their wedding. I directed a question at the woman: "Do you love this man, and are you willing to commit yourself to him for the rest of your life?" After a pause, she confessed she didn't really love him! She didn't want to invest her life with him. They both had been so enamored with the idea of having a wedding, receiving gifts, and building a home and family, that they had ignored the fact that they didn't have a relationship of love. They realized that it would be wrong to marry without such a commitment and they broke their engagement.

People don't get married just so they can perform household chores, provide for a family, or cook meals. They get married because they are in love! In the same way, the Christian life is not merely a set of activities. Young adults don't become Christians just so they can go to church every Sunday, read their Bibles daily, and give money to the church! They become Christians because they come to love Jesus Christ. Christianity is a relationship. It's not a set of doctrines to believe, duties to perform, sins to avoid, or rituals to practice. Christianity is a relationship with a Person who loves you more than you'll ever comprehend and who wants you to love Him in return.

> YOUNG ADULTS DO NOT BECOME CHRISTIANS
> JUST SO THEY CAN GO TO CHURCH EVERY SUNDAY,
> READ THEIR BIBLES DAILY,
> AND GIVE MONEY TO THE CHURCH!
> THEY BECOME CHRISTIANS BECAUSE THEY COME
> TO LOVE JESUS CHRIST.
> CHRISTIANITY IS A *RELATIONSHIP*.

Jesus described the essence of the Christian life when He prayed, "This is eternal life: that they may know you, the only true God, and Jesus Christ whom you have sent" (John 17:3).

According to Jesus, eternal life is knowing God. This is not just head knowledge, or the collection of facts about God, but an intimate, growing, deepening relationship with Him.

The apostle John had the pleasure of coming to know Jesus in this way. In the Scripture below, notice the wonderful relationship that Jesus developed with John. Underline each act or statement that indicates a friendship between Jesus and John.

> "One of them, the disciple whom Jesus loved, was reclining next to him. Simon Peter motioned to this disciple and said, 'Ask him which one he means.' Leaning back against Jesus, he asked him, 'Lord, who is it?' " (John 13:23-25).

> "When Jesus saw his mother there, and the disciple whom he loved standing nearby, he said to his mother, 'Dear woman, here is your son,' and to the disciple, 'Here is your mother.' From that time on, this disciple took her into his home" (John 19:26-27).

> "The disciple whom Jesus loved said to Peter, 'It is the Lord!' " (John 21:7).

Did you notice the way John referred to himself when he wrote his Gospel? Modesty prevented him from mentioning his own name and so at times he used a designation for himself. He could have referred to himself as "the one who believed in God" or "the one who followed Jesus." Instead, he thought of himself in terms of his relationship with Jesus: "the one whom Jesus loved." What a profound way to look at yourself!

In the boxes below, check the descriptions that best describe your relationship with God.

❏ Intimate and personal   ❏ Distant   ❏ Growing
❏ A true friendship   ❏ Seldom talk   ❏ Cold and stale
❏ Broken relationship   ❏ Have little in common   ❏ Strangers
❏ One whom Jesus loves   ❏ Beginning friendship

Throughout the Scriptures God is presented as someone who seeks to have a love rela-tionship with people. God called Abraham His friend (Isaiah 41:8), and Scripture says God spoke to Moses "face to face, as a man speaks with his friend" (Exodus 33:11).

In the space below, list two things you're doing to enhance your love relationship with God. If you cannot do this, list one activity you could do to improve your relationship.

Is your relationship with God broken? Do you need to repent of anything in order to restore this relationship? If so, what is it?

Read the invitation God gave to Joshua in the Scripture below and underline the words or phrases that indicate a relationship between God and Joshua.

"No one will be able to stand up against you all the days of your life. As I was with Moses, so I will be with you; I will never leave you nor forsake you. Be strong and courageous, because you will lead these people to inherit the land I swore to their forefathers to give them. Be strong and very courageous. Be careful to obey all the law my servant Moses gave you; do not turn from it to the right or to the left, that you may be successful wherever you go. Do not let this Book of the Law depart from your mouth; meditate on it day and night, so that you may be careful to do everything written in it. Then you will be prosperous and successful. Have I not commanded you? Be strong and courageous. Do not be terrified; do not be discouraged, for the LORD your God will be with you wherever you go" (Joshua 1:5-9).

Go back and circle the phrases that indicate what Joshua was told to do.

What was the connection between Joshua's relationship with God and his assignment from God?

God works through His people on the basis of His relationship with them. Joshua was given an assignment, but it could only be carried out if he maintained his relationship with God. As Joshua obeyed God's instructions and meditated on His Word, God promised He would not leave Joshua and would give him success wherever he went. What an awesome invitation! Joshua's primary responsibility was to maintain his relationship with God, not to perform as a good general or a model administrator.

What's God currently leading you to do as a result of your relationship with Him?

Is there something you're currently attempting to do for God out of your own strength and not out of your relationship with Him? If so, what is it? How can you give it over to Him?

What did God say to you in your study today?

What will you do as a result?

GOD CALLS TO A DEFINITE CHOICE

> "Do not store up for yourselves treasures on earth, where moth and rust destroy, and where thieves break in and steal. But store up for yourselves treasures in heaven, where moth and rust do not destroy, and where thieves do not break in and steal" (Matthew 6:19-20).

In churches that we served as pastor, we often had young adults stand before the church to say they felt God leading them to train for full-time Christian service. Most of them went on to seminary or Bible college. One young man indicated God was speaking to him about becoming a pastor. He was a talented fellow, a gifted athlete, and a musician who was doing well in college. He volunteered for summer missions and served in a pioneer church for several weeks. He returned so excited about how God had used him during that summer! Then he had to decide whether to leave our city and travel to a distant seminary for his ministry training. While deliberating, he was offered a great chance to use his musical ability. He decided to delay going to seminary in order to pursue several of his other interests. He entered a business enterprise and it wasn't long before talk of preparing for the ministry ceased. One day a couple of years later, he was killed in a freak accident on the job. We don't know what God had in store for this man, but we sense that this life was tragically cut short before God could bring about His best.

God wants to give you abundant life (John 10:10b). However, He will not force His best upon you. To accept what the world provides rather than what God offers you is called "death" in Scripture. It means missing out on what God has in store for you. This may result in a lack of peace and fulfillment. It can mean anxiety, broken relationships, mediocrity, or even death. God speaks to His people, setting before them His ways. The choice, then, is between life (good) and death (evil).

GOD WANTS TO GIVE YOU ABUNDANT LIFE.
HOWEVER, HE WILL NOT FORCE HIS BEST UPON YOU.
TO ACCEPT WHAT THE WORLD PROVIDES
RATHER THAN WHAT GOD OFFERS YOU
IS CALLED "DEATH" IN SCRIPTURE.

Read Deuteronomy 30:11-20 and identify the two choices and the two consequences God's people had to choose.

Choice 1:

_____

Choice 2:

_____

Consequence 1:

_____

Consequence 2:

_____

According to this passage, how difficult is it for you to know God's will?

When God speaks, what are your choices?

What happens if you don't protect your relationship with God?

INVESTMENTS FOR A LIFETIME

A young man once shared with us that he was struggling between two directions for his life. On the one hand, he felt God had called him into full-time Christian ministry. He had been invited to lead a new Christian student group on a college campus. On the other hand, he had a burning desire to become wealthy. He felt certain that through real estate, he could become rich at a young age. He reasoned that with his wealth he could support many Christian causes. He chose to pursue his fortune. Everything went according to his plan until the real estate market crashed. He lost everything, including his family. He had chosen to invest in the temporal rather than the eternal, and he discovered how transitory the things of this world are.

Life is full of choices. The issue of how much of your life you will spend is already settled: 24 hours each day. How you spend it is another matter. How you respond to the invitations God gives you will determine the kind and quality of your life.

In the Scriptures below, notice what Jesus said about how you can invest your life.

> "The ground of a certain rich man produced a good crop. He thought to himself, 'What shall I do? I have no place to store my crops.' Then he said, 'This is what I'll do. I will tear down my barns and build bigger ones and there I will store all my grain and my goods. And I'll say to myself, 'You have plenty of good things laid up for many years. Take life easy; eat, drink and be merry.' But God said to him, 'You fool! This very night your life will be demanded from you. Then who will get what you have prepared for yourself?' This is how it will be with anyone who stores up things for himself but is not rich toward God" (Luke 12:16-21).

List what Jesus taught about investments and the investments that the rich fool made.

Jesus' Teaching	The Rich Fool
_____	_____
_____	_____
_____	_____
_____	_____
_____	_____
_____	_____

Jesus said to store up for yourself "treasures in heaven." That is, invest your life in things that have eternal value and won't pass away with time. Spiritual realities do not suffer decay as do physical possessions. To lead people to a personal relationship with Jesus Christ means that their eternity is immediately altered and a place in heaven is prepared as a result of what you did on earth.

In contrast, the rich fool in Luke 12 had made no preparation for eternity. Perhaps he planned to do so once his earthly concerns were dealt with, but because he did not have God's eternal perspective, he was oblivious to the fact that his life was about to come to an unexpected end. He had done what society praises. He had worked hard, harvested a good crop, and stored his grain. His barns were full and there wasn't enough room to store all his possessions. He expanded his operation so that he had enormous reserves of grain and goods. Now he could enjoy early retirement in ease and luxury. There was nothing wrong or evil about planning for his retirement, except that he had not first prepared for eternity. If he had known his life was to end soon, surely he would have ordered his priorities differently! That's why it's critical that you allow God to guide you in the way you invest your life. Only He knows what lies ahead and how you can lay up treasures for yourself which will make you rich toward God.

What's one way you're tempted to invest your life in temporal rather than eternal pursuits?

How could this keep you from experiencing God's best?

What changes do you need to make in the way you're investing your life?

What did God say to you during your study today?

What will you do as a result?

2

CHARACTER: THE BASIS FOR YOUR FUTURE

"Above all else, guard your heart, for it is the wellspring of life" (Proverbs 4:23).

DANIEL WAS A YOUNG MAN with a promising future. He had done well in school and now powerful people were vying for his services. Moving far from home, he found himself surrounded by every imaginable temptation. Daniel had been raised in a religious home with strict morals and values. Now influential people were telling him that if he would compromise just a little, he could obtain wealth and power beyond his wildest dreams. It seemed he had everything to gain and nothing to lose. To refuse to go along could seriously harm his future. The potential for success seemed enormous; the possibility of being caught, remote. What would you do?

Of course, we know what Daniel chose to do. The Bible reveals that despite all the temptations and threats he received, "Daniel resolved not to defile himself" (Daniel 1:8). What amazing integrity! He didn't need his parents looking over his shoulder or his pastor checking up on him; he had developed a spiritual strength of character so firm that even the most tantalizing temptations couldn't shake his convictions. Do you have that kind of integrity before God and with people?

OUR FUNCTION: AN ASSIGNMENT BASED ON CHARACTER

> "The good man brings good things out of the good stored up in his heart,
> and the evil man brings evil things out of the evil stored up in his heart.
> For out of the overflow of his heart his mouth speaks" (Luke 6:45).

Newspapers occasionally report on lawyers who betray their clients' trust and illegally use money that's not their own. Others bill their clients falsely or mishandle investment funds. The paradox is that these are the same people who've spent years carefully studying the laws of their land. Apparently for some, their goal has been simply to obtain a job with wealth and prestige. Their studies obviously had no effect on their character.

In God's eyes not only is the destination important, but so is the journey. The activities of our lives are God's means for helping change us into the people He wants us to become. Jesus told John, "Come, follow me … and I will make you …" (Mark 1:17). Jesus told John He would transform him into a fisher of men if he would follow Him as a disciple. God is not as concerned with our activities as He is with our character, which motivates our actions.

When God revealed Himself to the Israelites while they were slaves in Egypt, He did so for a purpose. He rescued them from slavery and brought them to Himself so they might enjoy freedom as God's people. Read in Exodus 19:5-6 what God wanted to do with His people.

What did God want for His people based on Exodus 19:5-6?

In the same passage, what did the Israelites have to do to become what God wanted?

God in His grace chose to make the Israelites His "treasured possession." He wanted to make them a "kingdom of priests and a holy nation." There would never be another nation like this. This rag-tag collection of uneducated, demoralized slaves was going to become a unique group. Every person would have a special relationship with God and would be His ambassador to the world. God was going to accomplish this by making a commitment to them and giving them careful instructions about how to live in order to be acceptable to Him.

CHARACTER DICTATES CONDUCT

What you're made of determines how you act. Trustworthy individuals are elevated to positions of responsibility. Conversely, people in authority can fall, losing everything because of a serious character flaw. In Scripture, the core of your personality commonly is referred to as the heart. This is where you make moral decisions and hold your values. Your spontaneous actions reveal your inner self. For example, if you automatically tell the truth, then you're by nature a truthful person. However, if you sometimes struggle with telling the truth as you consider what would benefit you the most, you're not an honest person. You have a serious flaw that could ultimately lead to ruin. What you do instinctively in any situation is your character. Jesus was far more concerned with people's hearts than He was with their actions. Notice His observation in Luke 6:43-45.

According to Jesus, how do you recognize different trees?

How can you identify a "good tree"?

From where do your actions come?

Is it possible to be a "good" tree and produce "bad" fruit? Explain.

Jesus taught that a tree is identified by the fruit it produces. Likewise, young adults may claim to be one thing but the "fruit" of their lives will shout the opposite.

Read the Scriptures below and circle the behaviors Jesus said were incompatible in a person's life.

"Why do you call me, 'Lord, Lord,' and do not do what I say?" (Luke 6:46).

"No one who is born of God will continue to sin, because God's seed remains in him; he cannot go on sinning, because he has been born of God" (1 John 3:9).

"Anyone who hates his brother is a murderer, and you know that no murderer has eternal life in him" (1 John 3:15).

"If anyone has material possessions and sees his brother in need but has no pity on him, how can the love of God be in him?" (1 John 3:17).

"If we claim to have fellowship with him yet walk in the darkness, we lie and do not live by the truth" (1 John 1:6).

"Do not love the world or anything in the world. If anyone loves the world, the love of the Father is not in him" (1 John 2:15).

Read Luke 6:43-45 again. List practices or attitudes that can't be part of a Christlike character.

Review your list for any trait that's part of your own character.

How would you describe your character in light of these verses?

Do you see the importance of your heart's condition? If your heart is right and your character is Christlike, certain actions naturally occur and others are noticeably absent.

Whether at work or at church, most young adults like to feel that their peers or superiors have enough confidence to trust them with an important job. With God, any task He gives you is significant! God is far more concerned, however, with your character than He is with your assignment.

Here is some thought-provoking counsel given by others.

> "Do not pray for easy lives. Pray to be stronger . . . ! Do not pray for tasks equal to your powers. Pray for powers equal to your tasks! Then the doing of your work shall be no miracle. But you shall be a miracle."
> Phillips Brooks, *Twenty Sermons*[1]

> "If your place is not great enough to suit you, make it so. The minister who is unable to make a place great is too weak to hold a great one."
> L. R. Scarborough, *With Christ After the Lost*[2]

NO SHORTCUTS TO CHARACTER
God assigns tasks according to what He sees in your heart.

What is God asking you to do right now? How faithful are you being to that task?

Do you know others whose primary focus is to find the easiest path to their goal? What affect might this have on them in the long-run?

Cutting corners and taking shortcuts in life shortchanges skills, knowledge, and personal growth that will affect God's assignment for His children. We can't tell you how many people have come to us in great frustration, sharing how they were careless with their studies in college or seminary or in their first job because they simply were pushing to get through to the next big thing. Then God began speaking to them about His plans for them but the door had closed. They hadn't learned the lessons they should have. They had not become all they should and now their assignments from God were limited.

This kind of person is often quick to abandon his or her current assignment when a tempting offer comes along. We've known young adults who were offered jobs while still in college. In their eagerness to jump to the finish line, they dropped out of school, telling themselves, *I don't need to keep studying. I have a job now!* Many times their careers ended in failure, partly because they had inadequate training. An additional reason, however, is their character. It's such that they jump at every new and seemingly easier opportunity that comes along and never give God the time to build into them the strength that can withstand the difficult tests that are sure to come.

God assigns tasks according to what He sees in your heart. Right now, how big would God's assignment be for you?

What could God be teaching you now as He prepares you for greater things?

On what area of your character is God working?

What did God say to you during your study today?

What will you do as a result?

OUR FRUIT: A TRANSFORMING WORK OF GOD

> "Being confident of this, that he who began a good work in you will carry
> it on to completion until the day of Christ Jesus" (Philippians 1:6).

In 1463 the sculptor Agostino di Duccio was commissioned to produce a statue. He was given a large slab of marble upon which he began to chisel his masterpiece. Tragically, however, his apprentice made a careless mistake that left the marble disfigured. Agostino was horrified at the sight of the damaged stone and did everything in his power to restore it, to no avail. This beautiful, unfinished piece of marble was declared hopelessly ruined. Rejected by its master, the rock stood in a courtyard for the next 38 years.

In 1501 a 25-year-old artist named Michelangelo came upon the abandoned stone. When he looked at the marble he did not see a broken piece of rock, but incredible potential. All he had to do was chisel away anything that did not look like a masterpiece. When he was finished, there stood the awesome statue of *David,* one of the greatest sculptures of all time!

Many young adults find themselves broken and scarred. Perhaps difficult home lives or painful events in the past have left them damaged or incomplete. They may bear the stains of past sins they committed or were committed against them. There may be scars that run deep as a result of sinful lifestyles. The good news is that Christ wants to fashion us into a divine masterpiece.

PETER THE ROCK

It's interesting to see how Jesus gave some of His disciples "nicknames" to illustrate their character. He named Simon "Peter," meaning "rock." You've probably heard the expression "steady as a rock"; Peter's early career as a disciple was anything but steady! Nevertheless, Jesus took Peter through a thorough process of character development.

Contrast the following passages that reflect growth in Peter's character over time as he walked with Jesus.

Read Matthew 14:29-31.   Now read Acts 12:6-11.
Read Luke 22:60-62.   Now read Acts 4:13,18-20.

What changes do you notice in the character of Peter?

Is there one area of your character you feel God has changed? What is it?

What aspect(s) of your character do you think Jesus would like to change?

As a new convert, Peter was sincere, but suffered a shallow faith. He was willing to impulsively step out on the water to meet Jesus, but as soon as he realized what he had done he began to doubt. Later, he trusted God so completely that he slept soundly the night before his scheduled execution and escaped a maximum security prison without expressing the slightest doubt! As a new convert, Peter was someone who crumbled under pressure. When a servant girl asked him if he was a disciple of Jesus, Peter became so fearful he denied it, cursing. Later, under the fiercest threats by the most powerful men in the nation, he stood firm in his loyalty to Christ.

The difference was Christ and the changes He made in Peter's character. When Jesus met Peter, He saw beyond what Peter was like at that moment to what he could become by the transforming work of the Spirit of God. While it is true that Christ loves you just the way you are, He also loves you despite the way you are. If God accepted you without expecting you to change, that would not be genuine love. Christ loves you and is determined to make you reach your full potential as a Spirit-filled child of God. As Christ develops your character, the Heavenly Father will continue to expand your assignment.

PAUL THE PHARISEE

The apostle Paul experienced the reality that Christ can take the most hardened sinner and transform him into a saint. In the next Scripture, notice what he said about himself.

"You have heard of my previous way of life in Judaism, how intensely I persecuted the church of God and tried to destroy it. I was advancing in Judaism beyond many Jews of my own age and was extremely zealous for the traditions of my fathers" (Galatians 1:13-14).

What did Paul identify as those things that reflected his character before he became a Christian?

If you had known Paul at that time, would you have thought it likely that he would become a devout Christian leader and church starter? Why or why not?

Paul was a sanctimonious Pharisee. He was fiercely competitive and strived to surpass his peers in his religious zeal. He callously imprisoned Christians and had some put to death. Paul saw nothing wrong with his character and thought he was living a faultless life. He was ambitiously using the system to advance his career and reach the pinnacle of power among his people. This wasn't the kind of person whom you expect to become a Christian martyr, let alone invite home for dinner! Yet notice the change Christ brought about in his life as illustrated in excerpts from one of Paul's letters.

"I f anyone is in Christ, he is a new creation; the old has gone, the new has come!" (2 Corinthians 5:17).

According to this verse, what changes do you detect in Paul's character?

What did Paul say was the reason for his change of character?

Few lives mentioned in Scripture underwent as dramatic a turnaround as Paul's. Christ transformed him into someone totally different from who he had been. Paul's life became a miracle of God's grace.

You'll never be able to develop a Christlike character on your own. Despite your best efforts, and all the self-help books you might read, only Christ can produce a Christlike character. This is accomplished as the Holy Spirit works in your life.

Read the following fruit of the Spirit from Galatians 5:22-24. Write down one example of the Holy Spirit's activity in your life in each area.

> "The fruit of the Spirit is love, joy, peace, patience, kindness, goodness, faithfulness, gentleness and self-control. Against such things there is no law. Those who belong to Christ Jesus have crucified the sinful nature with its passions and desires. Since we live by the Spirit, let us keep in step with the Spirit. Let us not become conceited, provoking and envying each other" (Galatians 5:22-26).

Love:

Joy:

Peace:

Patience:

Kindness:

Goodness:

Faithfulness:

Gentleness:

Self-control:

What do you notice about what God is doing in your character?

The Holy Spirit is determined to produce spiritual fruit in your life. He won't force you to love or to be joyful, but if you allow Him, He'll mold you and remove harmful things from your life until, when He's finished, your character resembles that of Christ.

What did God say to you during your study today?

What will you do as a result?

OUR FOCUS: A HEART SEEKS

> " Above all else, guard your heart, for it is the wellspring of life. Put away perversity from your mouth; keep corrupt talk far from your lips. Let your eyes look straight ahead, fix your gaze directly before you. Make level paths for your feet and take only ways that are firm. Do not swerve to the right or the left; keep your foot from evil" (Proverbs 4:23-27).

The college students in our church used to hold an annual banquet. This was always a special time for the students, and everyone came dressed in their finest attire. One year, a slovenly stranger wandered into the banquet room and began visiting with the students. He obviously wasn't one of the group, and he began to make people uncomfortable. When the meal was served, the interloper found a seat and began eating with the others. The students did what they could to let this young man know that this was a private function, but he remained undaunted.

After the meal, a skit was performed. The sketch began with a scene in heaven in which God summoned an angel to go and investigate our college group. Suddenly this stranger appeared! He was the angel! He had been enlisted by the student president to test his reception by the rest of the group. Many felt embarrassed at the way they had been cold and unfriendly to the stranger. Although the students took pride in their friendliness, on this occasion when they were tested, they failed the exam!

How you respond in unguarded moments can be the best test of your character. Unexpected temptation can be devastating! You may think you have a holy life or that you are a loving person, but when the test comes, if you are unprepared you may discover the true nature of your heart. Heed the wise advice of the writer of Proverbs 4:23-27: "Above all else, guard your heart."

In your own words, list the things Proverbs 4:23-27 instructs to do.

Go back and circle the things you are currently doing.

There are at least three things that greatly affect your character. These are your values, friends, and habits. Consider the following carefully.

VALUES: KEEPING YOU ON TRACK

A young couple had dedicated their lives to full-time Christian service. They were training for the ministry for which they knew God was calling them. Since they both had jobs while they were in seminary, they decided a house would be a wise investment. They began acquiring furniture and appliances for their new home. Then they purchased a second car. The need to earn more money to pay their bills grew greater. First one of them, then the other, dropped out of school. The stress of trying to run the rat race of consumerism was so great that their marriage grew shaky. What happened? Instead of sticking to their priority of obeying God and finishing their education, they allowed material possessions to become their top priority and almost lost everything.

> THE THINGS THAT ARE MOST IMPORTANT TO YOU
> WILL BE TO WHAT YOU GIVE THE MAJORITY
> OF YOUR TIME, MONEY, AND ENERGY.
> THE THINGS YOUR HEART TREASURES ARE YOUR VALUES.

Jesus said, "Where your treasure is, there your heart will be also" (Matthew 6:21). The things that are most important to you will be to what you give the majority of your time, money, and energy. The things your heart treasures are your values. During your twenties you will establish values that will shape and determine your future. The challenge will be to place the utmost importance on God and what He wants for your life as opposed to the possessions, activities, and rewards the world offers. You need an undivided heart for the priorities of God.

This means that you can't pursue God's values and the world's values at the same time. Jesus said that if you "seek first his kingdom and his righteousness, and all these things will be given to you as well" (Matthew 6:33). That is, when your values are the same as God's, He will grant you everything you need for an abundant life.

Notice the contrast in the values of the rich young ruler, the woman, and the disciples in Luke 18:18-24 and Matthew 26:6-9.

What did the rich ruler value more than anything else? How do you know this?

How did Jesus deal with the young man who had values different from His own?

What was important to the woman? How can you tell?

What was important to the disciples? How can you tell?

The rich ruler professed to be devoted to God and His causes. Yet in his heart he really was dedicated to his money. Jesus saw through the pretense of devotion and asked the man to rid himself of that which had a higher value than following Him. This radical command by Jesus laid bare the man's true values so that Jesus and everyone listening could see the real treasure of his heart.

The woman treasured Jesus and her relationship with Him more than anything. Her most precious possession was easily poured out in exchange for being able to express her love to Jesus. The disciples, however, were still bound by a worldly set of values. They knew it was good to show affection for Jesus, but they also knew the cost of this expensive perfume. This was a battle of values being waged between what the world esteems and what's supremely important to God!

The reason your values are important is that they determine your actions. You may be deciding between two job offers. One job may afford you the time to invest in your family and volunteer at your church. The other may pay a much higher salary but require you to travel and have little time for anything but work. The values you hold will strongly influence which job you take. You may be faced with the opportunity to have an affair with a married person. If your primary value is "Have a good time at all costs," you may succumb to the temptation. If your value is "Maintain moral purity and commitments made to your spouse," you'll resist any activity that might make you compromise your values. You will even avoid the appearance of compromise. Without God-given values your life will be adrift in an ocean of loose morals and questionable values.

What is God saying to you about the values you hold?

YOUR FRIENDS: A SUBTLE INFLUENCE

A young man claimed that he witnessed to some friends every Saturday night. He said they loved to spend the evening working on and racing their cars. He believed he was exerting a positive influence on his friends. We asked him what difference he thought he was making. He confessed he hadn't made it to church himself in more than a month. He admitted he was simply too tired because of the late Saturday nights. It seemed his friends were doing a better job of influencing him! Few things can have a greater impact on your character than the friends you keep. One of the best gauges of your values can be your friends.

Notice the biblical wisdom concerning friends in the Scriptures below. Write in your own words the main truth of each verse.

> **"Blessed is the man who does not walk in the counsel of the wicked or stand in the way of sinners or sit in the seat of mockers" (Psalm 1:1).**

> **"Listen to advice and accept instruction, and in the end you will be wise" (Proverbs 19:20).**

> **"Do not make friends with a hot-tempered man, do not associate with one easily angered, or you may learn his ways and get yourself ensnared" (Proverbs 22:24-25).**

> **"An unfriendly man pursues selfish ends; he defies all sound judgment" (Proverbs 18:1).**

> **"A man of many companions may come to ruin, but there is a friend who sticks closer than a brother" (Proverbs 18:24).**

We encourage you to seek friends with godly values, who are not timid about challenging you if you begin to stray from God's will.

When you're with people who sincerely love the Lord, you will also grow to love God more. When you're around people who desire to live holy lives, you'll be challenged to strive to make your life holy as well.

How are your friends drawing you closer to God and His will for your life?

Use the following criterion to rate the influence your friends are having on you. Check all that apply.

My friends ...

❑ Care enough to confront me   ❑ Encourage me to be in church

❑ Lead balanced lives   ❑ Live uncompromising Christian lives

❑ Encourage my Scripture memory   ❑ Tempt me to compromise my beliefs

❑ Are critical   ❑ Model Christlike behavior

❑ Are unreliable   ❑ Take far more than they give

❑ Pray for me regularly   ❑ Lose their temper with me

❑ Encourage me to walk closely with God

How do your friends rate? Remember, your friends will generally reflect your values.

What's God saying to you about your current relationships?

HABITS CHANGE HEARTS

Once you recognize you have values that impact your behavior and you choose friends who affect your choices, a third area that influences your heart is your habits. Some habits are good and are known as disciplines. These may be study habits, exercise regimens, or regular church attendance. Other habits are bad and may be called addictions. These may include overeating, excessive attention to making money, or drug dependency. By observing your habitual behavior, people can soon determine what's most important in your life. You can alter your own character by allowing Jesus, through the Holy Spirit, to build healthy habits. For example, controlling your anger through the power of God eventually will carve an enduring niche of tenderness in your heart. After a while, you will respond calmly without having to work at it.

Character determines the course of your life. Good habits build a noble heart. Therefore, guard your heart. Using the verses below as your guide, list some habits that will establish a healthy heart.

> "Rejoice in the Lord always. I will say it again: Rejoice! Let your gentleness be evident to all. The Lord is near. Do not be anxious about anything, but in everything, by prayer and petition, with thanksgiving, present your requests to God. And the peace of God, which transcends all understanding, will guard your hearts and your minds in Christ Jesus. Finally, brothers, whatever is true, whatever is noble, whatever is right, whatever is pure, whatever is lovely, whatever is admirable—if anything is excellent or praiseworthy—think about such things. Whatever you have learned or received or heard from me, or seen in me—put it into practice. And the God of peace will be with you" (Philippians 4:4-9).

It's critical to guard your heart. When hearts are left unguarded, Christians face their greatest defeats. Don't let this happen to you.

What are some habits you could build into your life that would protect your heart? Check the habits you need to begin practicing.

☐ Daily quiet time   ☐ Regular church participation
☐ Regular prayer group   ☐ Regular Bible study
☐ Fasting   ☐ Scripture memory
☐ Sabbath day of rest   ☐ Attending Christian conferences
☐ Prayer partner   ☐ Listening to Christian music

List five activities on which you spend your free time in a given week. Prioritize them in order of the most time spent to the least. Exclude mandatory activities such as sleeping, eating, attending classes, and work time.

After evaluating the use of your time, what adjustments do you think God wants to make?

What's God saying to you about your habits?

What did God say to you during your study today?

What will you do as a result?

OUR FAITHFULNESS: A LITTLE LEADS TO A LOT

> "His master replied, 'Well done, good and faithful servant! You have been faithful with a few things; I will put you in charge of many things. Come and share your master's happiness!'" (Matthew 25:21).

Gerry was a college dropout in search of meaning and purpose. He had several areas in his life in which he needed Christ to give him victory. Gerry became involved in the college ministry at our church and ultimately gave his life to Christ. He faced a crisis almost immediately after his baptism because his girlfriend ended their long-term relationship. In spite of his emotional turmoil, Gerry continued to seek the Lord's will for his life. About that time, a native Indian church sent word to our church that its elderly pastor needed someone to come and help him. Gerry volunteered to drive 200 miles each week in a vehicle held together by baling wire and hockey tape in order to minister to that place! When the native pastor resigned, the church called 24-year-old Gerry to be their pastor.

Five years later Gerry felt called to go to seminary. He moved, with his wife and two toddlers, back to the city and earned his college degree. During that time he was asked to begin a new church in the city; so, while attending college and providing for his family, he pastored a mission church. When that church called a full-time pastor, Gerry was invited to spend his summer starting another church in a small town several hours away. That fall Gerry and his family packed their meager belongings and traveled 1,500 miles to the nearest seminary to prepare for ministry. During his second year he was called as pastor of a small church two hours away. He moved to be near the church. This meant he had to arise at 5:00 a.m. to commute to his seminary classes two days a week. After three years of hard work in a challenging church, Gerry graduated from seminary and was invited to go as a missionary to Quebec, Canada. Quebec is one of the most unevangelized regions in the world today. For the next four years Gerry worked faithfully in that difficult mission field. He next received a call from his denomination to direct its ethnic work throughout the nation.

Today Gerry serves as his denomination's national leader. He bears only a faint resemblance to the scruffy university student he once was. As you might imagine, God has developed him into one of His effective servants. What made the difference in Gerry's life? His faithfulness. Gerry was always faithful in a little and God was correspondingly faithful to entrust him with more.

What was the criterion for Gerry being entrusted with more responsibility?

Faithfulness is a character trait that's highly praised by God. You might not think you have many talents to offer God or many skills to put into His service, but you can be faithful. Jesus indicated that in the time of judgment it will be a person's faithfulness that will be praised. Read Matthew 25:21.

What was the basis of the master's praise of his servant?

What effect did the servant's faithfulness have on his master?

Jesus' standard for rewarding His children with greater knowledge of God or more responsibility from God rests on the level of trustworthiness in which they handle small responsibilities God has given. If you can be faithful in little tasks, He will trust you with greater assignments. If you don't treat each date with integrity, then God may be reluctant to give you a permanent marriage partner. If you're faithful in wisely using the little money you have, He may bless you with more. If you treat each friendship God gives you with care, He will expand your circle of friends.

God is consistent in the way He relates to people. For example, someone may decide to enter seminary and train to be a pastor after being a Christian only a few months. However, God may say, "First join a regular Bible study at your church and learn some fundamental truths from My Word and then, when you have faithfully obeyed My Word in your life, I will prepare you to be an encouragement to others." God knows that your character and walk with Him may not be strong enough to handle any more responsibility than you currently have. If God has given you a small assignment, don't be discouraged. Recognize it as a time of testing to see if you are prepared for a larger one.

What might you conclude if God never gave you a larger assignment than what you have now?

A FRUSTRATED STUDENT

There was a young woman who was constantly experiencing financial distress. She could never hold onto a job for long. She complained that she always had difficult, unsympathetic bosses.

Finally, someone pointed out that it might not be her boss who had the problem. Rather, her poor job skills and lax work ethic may have been the real culprits for her unemployment blues. It had not dawned on her that because she hadn't been trustworthy in her work, God wasn't honoring her with anything better.

FAITHFULNESS EXAM

Take the following simple quiz. Be as honest as you can.

1. How faithful have you been with God's Word? Do you study it regularly and obey it consistently? ❏ Yes ❏ No
2. How faithful are you in prayer? Do you pray regularly? ❏ Yes ❏ No

3. How faithful are you with God's people? Are you an active member of a local church? Do you participate in the weekly activities of your church? ❑ Yes ❑ No

4. How faithful are you at being on mission with God? Are you always watching to see where He is at work? Are you involved in ministry with Him? ❑ Yes ❑ No

5. Are you a faithful witness? Do you regularly share your beliefs with those God brings across your path? ❑ Yes ❑ No

6. Are you faithful with your finances? Do you spend your money wisely? Do you invest it in God's kingdom or only on yourself? ❑ Yes ❑ No

7. Are you faithful with your schooling or job duties? Do you strive to do your best and to be diligent with those tasks? ❑ Yes ❑ No

8. Are you a faithful friend? Are you the kind of person people desire to have as a friend? ❑ Yes ❑ No

9. Have you been faithful with the family heritage God may have given you? Do you uphold the integrity of the Christian name that was passed on to you? ❑ Yes ❑ No

10. Have you been a careful caretaker of the body God has given you? ❑ Yes ❑ No

11. Has your Christian college group found you to be reliable in all they've asked you to do? ❑ Yes ❑ No

What did God say to you during your study today?

What will you do as a result?

OUR FAILURE: THE GOD OF SECOND CHANCES

> "If we confess our sins, he is faithful and just and will forgive us our sins
> and purify us from all unrighteousness" (1 John 1:9).

We have met with many individuals and couples as they wept and shared how they had forfeited God's best for their lives. It might be a young man confessing his moral impurity; or a young woman who had not been diligent in her job duties and lost out on a promotion; or a young man in bondage to addictive behaviors. The painful question is always eventually asked: "Have I blown it? Does God give a second chance? Could God use someone like me?"

Read Romans 8:28,35-39. According to these verses, what can separate you from the love of God?

Can failure separate you from the love of God? Explain your response.

Is there anything in your life that God cannot work for good? How much is included in "all things" in verse 28?

Scripture is clear. Nothing can separate you from the love of God. Even your worst failure is no obstacle to the love of God. That doesn't mean you won't face consequences or God's discipline. It does mean that God will continue to love you and seek to bring about His best in your life despite whatever setbacks result from your failures. God's assignment may change, but His love for you was forever settled on the cross and it will never change.

Have you experienced failure in your Christian life? Describe one area where you think you've failed.

The wonderful thing about the Bible is that it's candid about the failures of men and women. If you ever think Christians are perfect, just read the Bible!

DAVID THE MURDERER

There probably is no one in the Bible who had a more intimate relationship with God than David. Yet, David committed some of the most despicable sins recorded in Scripture. When David should have been leading his army, he chose to allow his servant Joab to take his place (2 Samuel 11:1). While idling away his time, David committed adultery with Bathsheba. If that weren't a grievous enough sin, David subsequently had Bathsheba's husband Uriah murdered so he could marry her. What a horrendous resumé of moral and spiritual failure: shunning his responsibility, theft, adultery, deception, and murder!

The prophet Nathan's scathing condemnation was earth-shattering to David as he heard his sins denounced by the man of God (2 Samuel 12:7-9). Throughout Psalm 51 (read this carefully), you see the absolute brokenness and contrition David felt. Despite David's genuine repentance, God allowed some severe consequences of his sins, which he endured the rest of his life (2 Samuel 12:10-14). Nevertheless, God forgave David's sin and loved and blessed him in many ways.

Not wanting to sin against God in that way again, David prayed. Read his prayer in the following Scripture.

"Search me, O God, and know my heart; test me and know my anxious thoughts. See if there is any offensive way in me, and lead me in the way everlasting" (Psalm 139:23-24).

PETER THE DENIER

Peter boasted of his courage and loyalty to Christ (Matthew 26:33), yet before the night was over he would commit the classic failure of all recorded history! Peter began by falling asleep, in spite of Jesus' repeated pleas for him to pray with Him (Matthew 26:36-46). Later, while Peter was following Jesus from a distance, a servant girl recognized him. When asked if he was a follower of Jesus, he denied it. Peter publicly denied he knew Jesus three times, the last time with a curse (Matthew 26:69-75).

Luke described the result of Peter's failure. Read Luke 22:60-62. How devastating that look from Jesus must have been! How deeply ashamed Peter must have felt. Yet, Jesus forgave him. Notice how gently and completely Jesus restored Peter (John 21:15-17). God later allowed Peter to preach the first sermon after Pentecost, which resulted in 3,000 people being added to the church (Acts 2:41). Peter's second sermon brought another 2,000 men to the church (Acts 4:4). God used Peter in incredible ways, completely forgiving and overcoming his earlier failure.

THOMAS THE DOUBTER

The disciple Thomas was not present when the risen Christ appeared to the other disciples (John 20:24). The fact that all the other disciples were there may indicate it was a meeting Thomas had chosen to miss. When he heard the animated reports from the disciples who had seen Jesus, Thomas responded with obvious doubt, "so the other disciples told him, 'We have seen the Lord!' But he said to them, 'Unless I see the nail marks in his hands and put my finger where the nails were, and put my hand into his side, I will not believe it'" (John 20:25). Even when all the other disciples believed Jesus and were excited about His presence, Thomas remained steadfast in his lack of faith.

Then Jesus appeared. He approached Thomas and showed him His hands and side. He saw the scars where Jesus had shed His blood for him, and Thomas could only respond, "My Lord and my God!" (John 20:28). Jesus restored Thomas to a place of faith in Him, and we never hear of him doubting Jesus again.

Your failures never catch Jesus by surprise. He is always prepared to respond to them. His love is never so overwhelmed by your failure that He doesn't continue to reach out to you. How should you respond to God when you fail? You might begin by claiming the verses below.

"Call to me and I will answer you and tell you great and unsearchable things you do not know" (Jeremiah 33:3).

"If we confess our sins, he is faithful and just and will forgive us our sins and purify us from all unrighteousness" (1 John 1:9).

What must you do for God to respond to your questions?

What must you do to have your sins forgiven?

Do you think this means God will forgive all your sins? Why or why not?

How did God respond to the failures of David, Peter, and Thomas?

How will God respond to your failures?

I've had the wonderful experience of seeing God take broken and sinful people and, by His grace, forgive and transform them into men and women of God. Only God could transform these lives! Perhaps you think there are things about your life that will prevent God from ever using you for His kingdom. Remember, nothing can separate you from the love of God!

What did God say to you during your study today?

What will you do as a result?

3

CAREER: A VEHICLE FOR GOD'S PURPOSES

"Commit to the LORD whatever you do, and your plans will succeed"
(Proverbs 16:3).

THERE WAS A FASCINATING EPISODE on the original *Star Trek* TV series titled "Tomorrow Is Yesterday." In it the crew of the U.S.S. Enterprise was thrown into a time warp and suddenly found themselves hovering above the United States during the 1960s. The U.S. Air Force immediately dispatched intercept aircraft to investigate. When the jet flown by Captain John Christopher began to break apart, the Enterprise "beamed" him aboard to save his life. Once aboard the starship, the amazed pilot was given a tour of the futuristic spaceship. To Christopher's dismay, however, Captain Kirk informed him that because he had seen the future, he could not be allowed to return to Earth. If he were to return, Kirk explained, he could use his new knowledge and alter the course of history. Desperately trying to persuade Captain Kirk that he should be sent home, Christopher countered by saying, "But then my disappearance would change something, too!" At this Spock shook his head. "I have run a computer check on all historical tapes," he said. "They show no record of any relevant contribution by John Christopher."

Imagine being plucked from the earth and having to justify the value of your life to humankind before you were allowed to return. What evidence would you cite to prove your life made any difference?

DEVELOPING YOUR RELATIONSHIP

"The LORD was with Joseph and he prospered" (Genesis 39:2).

One of the most frequent questions we hear from young adults is: "How do I know if God is calling me to be a pastor? Or a missionary? Or a teacher? Or a lawyer?" They are asking the wrong question. God doesn't necessarily call you to one, life-long job. He does call you to a relationship that lasts for eternity. God calls you to a relationship, and then out of that relationship, He guides you to a career. Just as Jesus "called" John to "come, follow Me," so your calling as a Christian is to follow Jesus wherever He leads you. Your job is simply an expression of God's current activity in your life. Your career may change several times, but your relationship with God is eternal. Your jobs have no eternal significance in and of themselves; they are vehicles of God's eternal purposes when you are rightly relating to Him.

Read the following passages and indicate the places where God was working in Joseph and through Joseph.

Career 1: Genesis 37:2

Career 2: Genesis 39:1-2

Career 3: Genesis 39:20-23

Career 4: Genesis 41:39-45

Which career do you think God wanted him to have? Why do you think God allowed Joseph to have so many different jobs?

Joseph originally was a shepherd because that was the family business. He then became manager of a large household and excelled at his work. Next he was a prison administrator. Finally, he became chief supervisor over an entire nation. That was quite a climb up the ladder! Which job did God want him to do? All of them. God led him to every position. Joseph's responsibility was to relate to God in obedience in whatever job he was assigned. As you walk with God, He may bring you through several jobs that provide different opportunities to serve Him and to grow in your relationship with Him.

Joseph trusted God implicitly, so God used him in His eternal plan. It was critical for Joseph to have a key position in the nation so God could use him to save thousands of Hebrews from starvation by bringing them to Egypt. Thus, God worked through Joseph and his career to build a holy nation for Himself.

As you prepare for a career, how are you maintaining a close relationship with God? In what ways is this affecting your career planning?

How has God begun to show you ways He might use you in a job to make a difference for His kingdom?

Are you willing to obey the next thing God tells you even if you cannot see what God has in mind for your future? What fears and/or dreams do you need to let go of in order to follow God's plan for you?

AN EXAMPLE FROM HENRY

People have asked me, "How did you know you were called to the job you're doing?" I answer that I never have felt called primarily to a job, but I have felt called to a relationship. As a young adult, I had several jobs, even working on a fishing boat. My first church job was leading music and working with education programs. Later, that same congregation asked me to become their pastor. I went on to be the pastor at two other churches. After that, I became a director of missions for an association of churches and still later I was asked to work for my national denomination. Which job did God want me to do? All of them! God was never as concerned with my particular job as He was that I walk with Him and listen to His voice. Don't let yourself get so hung up with a particular job that you neglect your relationship with God. Each place of service is an opportunity for God to fulfill His purposes through you.

DON'T LET YOURSELF GET SO HUNG UP
WITH A PARTICULAR JOB THAT YOU NEGLECT
YOUR RELATIONSHIP WITH GOD.
EACH PLACE OF SERVICE IS AN OPPORTUNITY
FOR GOD TO FULFILL HIS PURPOSES THROUGH YOU.

CAREER OR RELATIONSHIP?

While I (Richard) served as a pastor, I received a call from Bill, a church member. He worked with the government, made a good salary, and had plans for a comfortable retirement within five years. On this day, however, Bill had been informed that his position was being relocated to a town two hours away. God had given Bill a significant ministry in our church, and he knew he could not continue this work if he moved. Bill realized that refusing the transfer would mean forfeiting his job and losing the retirement income he had earned over many years. I clearly remember the service where he stood before the church to share his decision. He said his relationship to Christ was more important to him than any job. He chose to forfeit his employment and trust God to provide for his needs, allowing him to continue serving the church. The church prayed, and God did provide another job with the government, allowing him to retain his retirement. Bill continues to serve the Lord faithfully in his church today, and many people have come to know the Lord as a result.

God doesn't always require us to make such dramatic choices, but He does insist that we place our relationship with Him above anything else in our lives and trust Him with our future. With Him our future is secure as God accomplishes His purposes through us.

Do you think you could give up your job if Christ asked you to for His sake? Is your relationship with Christ more important to you than your career? Why or why not?

What did God say to you during your study today? What will you do as a result?

TRUSTING GOD'S PLAN

> "'I know the plans I have for you,' declares the LORD, 'plans to prosper you and not to harm you, plans to give you hope and a future'" (Jeremiah 29:11).

On June 30, 1859, more than 25,000 curious spectators gathered along the edge of Niagara Falls, staring incredulously at a tightrope stretched across the waterway, with no safety net below. Suddenly, 5-foot, 5-inch acrobat Jean Francois Gravelet approached the rope. He called himself the Great Blondin. He carried a 27-foot balancing pole as he stepped on to the tightrope. Despite several tense moments, Blondin managed to walk across the rope. He then began a series of death-defying stunts that left the audience spellbound. He carried a camera and tripod out to the middle of the rope to take a picture of the amazed crowd. He sat on a chair on the tightrope. He rode a bicycle, stood on his head, crossed while blindfolded, and pushed a wheelbarrow across!

After these incredible stunts, he challenged the baffled crowd: "How many of you believe I could carry a man on my back across this tightrope?" After viewing his remarkable antics, they readily acknowledged that Blondin was fully capable. Then came the unsettling question: "Which one of you wants to be that man?" Despite all their affirmations, no one was willing to risk his life. Blondin offered a substantial reward, but there were no takers.

Eventually, he enlisted volunteer Henry Colcord to be his passenger. Colcord did indeed ride successfully on his back, but only after being convinced of Blondin's reliability in the following way: Blondin took Colcord to a room where a beam was placed six inches above the ground. Blondin stood on the beam and challenged Colcord to push him off. Although Colcord pushed and pulled with all his might, Blondin's strength and balance were such that Colcord could not dislodge him. Colcord finally was convinced he could trust Blondin with his life.[1]

Young adults sometimes share the same mind-set as the crowd watching Blondin. They are quick to agree that God is almighty and can do anything He desires. They will affirm that God can provide a job and meet their needs. But then God asks them to leave the safety of the shore and step onto the tightrope! That's where faith is put to the test. Your faith in God is not proven by what you say, but by what you do. You could piously proclaim that you believe God can provide for all your needs, but when you cannot find a summer job, you do not have money for rent or tuition, or your car breaks down, you have the opportunity to demonstrate your faith.

GOD HAS A PLAN

In this complex and fast-paced world it's easy to become discouraged about the prospect of finding a meaningful career. Technology is progressing so rapidly that in a matter of months one can become deficient in the latest skills and knowledge required for one's work. High unemployment rates make for stiff job competition. Companies are downsizing and laying off long-time employees, making job security a thing of the past. Of course, as bleak as the job market sometimes appears, God is perfectly capable of guiding your life so you are effective for Him in the workplace. A verse that has encouraged many job-seekers is Jeremiah 29:11.

Do you believe God has a plan for your life? How does reading Jeremiah 29:11 affect that view?

What do you sense God wants to do with your life?

Do you believe God can provide a job and opportunities to serve Him in the workplace? What might those opportunities look like?

Have you placed your future and career in God's hands? Will you? How have you?

The people to whom Jeremiah was writing were in a hopeless situation. They were prisoners of the Babylonians, the international superpower of their day. They had no control over their education or job opportunities. From a human standpoint the Israelites' future appeared bleak. Yet God said if they would trust Him and maintain their relationship with Him, they could be assured of His plans for their lives and have tremendous hope for the future. Just as God had a plan for the Israelites' future, He also has one for you.

FAITH PLEASES GOD

The challenge you face is whether you believe God and what He says about your future. In the Scripture below, notice what the writer of Hebrews taught about faith in God.

> **"Without faith it is impossible to please God, because anyone who comes to him must believe that he exists and that he rewards those who earnestly seek him" (Hebrews 11:6).**

According to the Scripture you just read, can you please God while struggling to believe Him? Explain.

A lack of faith is more than a weakness or a shortcoming; it's inherently displeasing to almighty God. God says in His Word, "Everything that does not come from faith is sin" (Romans 14:23). God will place you in situations where you must trust Him. How will you respond when your life circumstances require trusting Him?

A STUDENT WHO OBEYED

Peter was a college student who believed God was telling him to get involved in a student summer missions program. He was willing to go but faced the serious dilemma that he would have no money to enroll in school in the fall. He understood what Philippians 4 says:

> **"My God will meet all your needs according to his glorious riches in Christ Jesus" (v. 19).**

He had already been denied a student loan, and if funds were not available in the fall, he would have to sit out a semester and find a job. He could not see the future, but he knew God could.

Peter chose to serve in summer missions. Upon his return, he faced a crisis in his belief in God because he did not have the money to enroll for the fall semester. Peter continued to believe that God would provide for his needs. On Wednesday evening Peter greeted me at church bubbling with excitement! Through miraculous circumstances, he had been granted a student loan which earlier had seemed unattainable. He had been offered a job that would perfectly fit his class schedule. Finally, a couple in the church had, under God's direction, invited him to live in their guest room rent free! Peter had been obedient and God was faithful, providing everything he needed.

If you never have to trust God, the people who watch your life will not see God at work and you will not have the opportunity to please God by your faith.

How have you displayed trust in God to provide for the following.
My financial needs:
My current/future career:
My health:
My future/current spouse:
My parents and family:

Has God put you in a circumstance where you are being forced to trust Him? If so, what is it?

What have you been learning about trusting God lately?

What did God say to you during your study today?

What will you do as a result?

HEARING GOD'S VOICE

> "The man who enters by the gate is the shepherd of his sheep.
> The watchman opens the gate for him, and the sheep listen to his voice.
> He calls his own sheep by name and leads them out" (John 10:2-3).

We talked one afternoon with a young man who had a promising future. He was trying to decide whether to enter law school or enroll in a theological seminary to prepare for Christian service. Was one career more important than the other? Which one was God telling him to do? Which one was his own wishful thinking? One would involve remaining at the same school with his friends; the other would require him to relocate to a different state. These issues were heavy on his mind as he sought to know for certain what God wanted him to do. We encouraged him that only as he related closely to God would he be able to hear God's voice and know his next assignment.

This kind of decision-making is not uncommon for young adults. With just one life to live, decisions about where to spend your working life are critical. A wrong choice could lead to years of drudgery, wasting years toiling at jobs that seem to make little difference to the world around you. It is vital that you clearly know when God is speaking. You will only be able to hear His voice as you develop a relationship with Him.

There's a heresy being taught today that God doesn't have a specific will for your life but is pleased to bless you as long as you don't sin. The Bible doesn't support this viewpoint. The moment you become a Christian, you accept the lordship of Jesus Christ and He sets the agenda for your life. When a job offer or career opportunity comes along, there are at least four ways to determine God's will as revealed by His Holy Spirit. We will look at the first two during today's lesson.

1. THE HOLY SPIRIT SPEAKS THROUGH THE BIBLE.

Suppose you receive an attractive job offer. Friends and family may encourage you to take the job, saying things such as "Look at how much money you would be making! That's a respectable company. You would get to travel in that job. You would get your own office. The extra benefits would be great! You could get valuable experience with that company. This job would look great on your resume. It would be close to home!" In spite of the attractiveness of the prospective job, you would be wise to use the Bible as a guide to determine God's direction. The Holy Spirit will guide you through biblical truths as well as specific Scriptures.

BIBLICAL TRUTHS

Read the following Scriptures and write a truth that could be applied as you consider finding a job. A truth after the first verse has been added as an illustration.

> **"The man of integrity walks securely, but he who takes crooked paths will be found out" (Proverbs 10:9).**
>
> Truth: *As long as I am honest and refuse to compromise my beliefs at work, I know God will honor me and protect me on the job.*
>
> Truth:

> **"Do you see a man skilled in his work? He will serve before kings; he will not serve before obscure men" (Proverbs 22:29).**
>
> Truth:

> **"Do not wear yourself out to get rich; have the wisdom to show restraint. Cast but a glance at riches, and they are gone, for they will surely sprout wings and fly off to the sky like an eagle" (Proverbs 23:4-5).**
>
> Truth:

I see at least five truths in these verses. *First, when the choice is between honoring God or obtaining a certain job, Scripture gives clear guidance as to what is most important.* We know people who refused high-paying jobs that would require them to compromise their integrity. In the competitive job market you face today, these pressures are sure to come and you will need to have integrity built firmly into your life.

A second truth is that it's good to work hard. We have had many people come to us and excitedly share about a job possibility that could make them well-off with only minimal effort on their part. We always caution them that when a job seems too good to be true, it probably is! Biblically, you're headed for trouble if your job choice is based on what will be the least demanding for you. Read Proverbs carefully and notice all it says about the consequences of laziness.

A third truth is that whatever job you have, you should commit it to the Lord. Could you wholeheartedly entrust the job you're considering to the Lord and would God be pleased with the work you would be doing? If you've committed your job to God, He will use it to bring glory to Himself.

Fourth, plan to be skilled in your work. Being a lackadaisical employee is despicable to God. Is the job you're considering or currently doing one in which you're skilled or could become skilled? Is it a job in which you will strive to do your best? Never settle for mediocrity in anything you do.

Finally, money isn't everything! There is nothing wrong with earning a good salary, but the wage rarely is the most important factor in job choice. If you put all your effort into achieving higher-paying jobs, you will "weary" yourself, only to discover that the pleasures of this world are fleeting and don't provide the peace that comes only from a relationship with God.

SPECIFIC SCRIPTURES

In addition to biblical truths, the Holy Spirit will speak to you through certain Scriptures to give specific direction to your life. God will never contradict His Word. That is, He will never tell you to do anything that is contrary to what He has said in Scripture. Sometimes He will direct you to certain verses to guide you.

For example, you may be deliberating whether to take a job as a waitress. In many ways it's a good job, but it requires you to work on Sundays. As you are praying and asking God what you should do, you turn in your Bible for your daily study and come to Hebrews 10:24-25.

Read what these verses say.

If this verse stands out as you read, what could God be saying?

As you reread these verses you sense that God is speaking to you. You remember the new Christians who are in the Bible study you lead on Sunday mornings and realize that it's far more important for you to be at church and encourage fellow believers than it is for you to take this particular job.

Has God been indicating through Scriptures what kind of job He would like you to have? What has He been saying?

2. THE HOLY SPIRIT SPEAKS THROUGH PRAYER.

A second way the Holy Spirit will guide you is through prayer. If you regularly present to God every major decision you are facing, He will impress upon you what you should do. The Holy Spirit does this in several ways. If, each time you ask Him whether you should take a certain job, God gives you a sense of divine peace, that will be one way God affirms the job. If, however, every time you pray you experience an uneasy spirit, it may be that God is cautioning you from proceeding further with that opportunity.

The Holy Spirit also will communicate with you by bringing Scriptures to your mind as you pray. For example, you might have the opportunity to work for a company that will treat you extremely well as an employee. However, the company may generate products you know are immoral. You know you would have difficulty promoting the product, but you also reason that you might be a Christian witness in your workplace. As you are praying about this decision, the Holy Spirit suddenly brings a passage of Scripture vividly to mind, such as 1 Corinthians 8:

> "If what I eat causes my brother to fall into sin, I will never eat meat again, so that I will not cause him to fall" (v. 13).

If you were suddenly reminded of this Scripture, what do you think the Holy Spirit might be saying about your job choice?

You may think your values and beliefs would not be adversely affected by your new work environment. You may even see how you could witness to others at work. Nevertheless, the Holy Spirit could be saying your employment for that particular company may have such a negative impact on others that it would do far more harm than good for your Christian witness. The Spirit knows all the consequences of your decision, for you and others, and may be cautioning you to consider more than your own needs in choosing a job.

IF YOU PUT ALL YOUR EFFORT INTO ACHIEVING HIGHER-PAYING JOBS, YOU WILL WEARY YOURSELF, ONLY TO DISCOVER THAT THE PLEASURES OF THIS WORLD ARE FLEETING AND DON'T PROVIDE THE PEACE THAT COMES ONLY FROM A RELATIONSHIP WITH GOD.

How intentional are you at listening for God to speak when you pray?

What has God been saying to you in your prayer times about the kind of work He wants you to do?

What did God say to you during your study today?

What will you do as a result?

FOLLOWING GOD'S LEADING

> "The Israelites went through the sea on dry ground, with a wall of water
> on their right and on their left" (Exodus 14:22).

Byron was a student of architecture who sincerely wanted to follow Christ. Jesus led him to Toronto, Canada's largest city and a place with a desperate need for the gospel. Byron found a job in a large architectural firm with excellent opportunities to use his training and talents. The more Byron became involved in God's work in that great city, however, the more he felt restricted by his company. God led him to quit his job and go into business for himself. Although this initially meant financial hardship and insecurity, it freed him to be an instrument of God in the metropolitan mission field. Today he is involved in starting a church that reaches out to business people who work in downtown Toronto, and God is blessing him and his work. Like Byron, God will guide you to invest your life in His eternal work.

Yesterday's lesson dealt with two ways God speaks to you through the Holy Spirit. Write them from memory in the space below.

3. THE HOLY SPIRIT SPEAKS THROUGH CIRCUMSTANCES.

There's a third way the Holy Spirit will guide you in your job search. This is through your circumstances. Circumstances alone can be confusing and must be evaluated in light of what the Spirit also says to you through the Bible, prayer, and the church. However, circumstances can help point you to God's will for your life.

SPIRITUAL MARKERS

Circumstances guide you if you pay attention to your spiritual markers, those key times in your life when you know God has clearly spoken and has guided you. Read Joshua 4:1-7.

In the Scripture you read, what did God want the people to do? Why?

The children of Israel had just witnessed a miracle. God, by His divine power, parted the Jordan River and allowed them to cross on dry land. God dramatically reminded His people that He was on their side and, if they would obey Him, He would give them victory. Since people tend to forget even the greatest acts of God, He commanded the Israelites to build a stone monument that would stand as a permanent reminder of His power.

You may have instances in your life when God clearly indicates His will. God spoke to you at your moment of salvation. God spoke to you as a child, as a teenager, and during key moments in your life. Although God is present to speak to you during your quiet times, there are points at which God's word will be extremely clear to you. During these moments, it is important that you build a spiritual "pile of stones." We call these spiritual markers. There are different ways to build spiritual markers. You can write what God said to you in a journal or write a note in your Bible (include the date). You may save special cards you received in the mail that God used to speak to you, or pictures of key events in your spiritual pilgrimage.

Spiritual markers are important because they help you understand what God is saying to you today. For example, Mike became a Christian at an early age. As a child, he attended a summer camp where God clearly spoke to him about missions. When Mike was a teenager, God used a sermon by a visiting missionary to affirm His calling to pursue international missions. When Mike reached college, God spoke powerfully to him during one of his quiet times and again sensitized his heart to world missions. Then, as he approached graduation, a friend invited Mike to join him in his business. This would require a commitment of several years, but the job would be extremely lucrative. Mike asked God what he should do. As he looked at his spiritual journal, he noticed that from the earliest time he heard God's voice, God had consistently guided him in the same direction: toward missions. As Mike plotted out what God had clearly said, he saw how contrary this career opportunity would be to all God had told him up to that point. His spiritual markers helped clarify God's will.

SPIRITUAL MARKERS ARE IMPORTANT BECAUSE THEY HELP YOU
UNDERSTAND WHAT GOD IS SAYING TO YOU TODAY.

Have you noted the spiritual markers in your life? What are some things you know God said to you ...

As a teenager: _____

As a college student: _____

As a young adult: _____

If you have not done so, record these in your journal or Bible. What pattern have you noticed in the things God has been saying to you?

How do your current career plans match what God has said to you previously?

OPEN DOORS CAN BE CONFUSING!

Few things are more confusing to people than open doors. An open door can be defined as any opportunity that presents itself to you. This can be a job offer, a proposal of marriage, or a major purchase. Many Christians assume that if God allows an opportunity to come, then it must be His will!

Read 2 Kings 20:12-18. What was the open door King Hezekiah faced?

In what ways did it appear attractive to enter?

What was wrong with this opportunity?

What was the consequence of entering this open door?

> CLOSED DOORS CAN BE JUST AS MISLEADING AS OPEN ONES.
> AT TIMES A DOOR CAN APPEAR TO BE CLOSED;
> ALTHOUGH YOU SENSE GOD WANTS YOU TO DO
> SOMETHING, IT SEEMS IMPOSSIBLE.

King Hezekiah jumped at the chance to show off to messengers of another country. Kings are always seeking alliances, and these messengers had come to him as friends. The problem was that in his eagerness to seize the opportunity, he sowed the seeds of Jerusalem's eventual destruction. These supposed friends reported all they saw to their king, and as a result, the king of Babylon eventually plundered Jerusalem.

Closed doors can be just as misleading as open ones. At times a door can appear to be closed; although you sense God wants you to do something, it seems impossible. Notice an apparent closed door that occurred as the children of Israel fled from the Egyptian army. Behind them was a fierce enemy; in front of them lay an impassable sea.

Read Exodus 14:10-13,21-22. How did the door the Israelites were facing appear to be closed?

Was it really closed? How did God open the door?

A DOOR CLOSED BY GOD

Paul faced a door that was closed by God.

Read this account in Acts 16:6-7. How were doors closed for Paul?

Paul sincerely wanted to evangelize Asia. He saw the tremendous need and he was willing to go. He had good intentions and desired to serve the Lord. God, however, had other plans for Paul. He gave Paul a vision telling him to go to Greece. God has the right to prevent you from going in one direction if there is something else He would rather have you do.

Not every opportunity that comes your way is from God. You must be sensitive to what the Holy Spirit is saying to you through your circumstances. Events in your life are neutral. It's what the Spirit says to you through those events that's important. Be sure to evaluate every open or closed door in light of what God has said to you through the Bible, prayer, and the people of God. Hearing God's voice in the midst of your activities, however, will depend on how closely you maintain your relationship with Him.

What has God been saying to you through your circumstances?

What open or closed doors have you been facing? How have you verified them with the Bible, prayer, and the people of God?

4. THE HOLY SPIRIT SPEAKS THROUGH THE CHURCH.

Your involvement in the church will be discussed further in session 6, but note that as you seek God's guidance concerning your career, your church can be a valuable instrument to guide you. Notice what the apostle Paul said about the church in this Scripture:

> "... so that there should be no division in the body, but that its parts should have equal concern for each other. If one part suffers, every part suffers with it; if one part is honored, every part rejoices with it. Now you are the body of Christ, and each one of you is a part of it" (1 Corinthians 12:25-27).

Notice how closely Paul said each church member should relate to the other. How will this intimacy between members affect you as you seek a job?

Paul was saying that members of a church should be so intimately connected that it's impossible for one to suffer without everyone feeling the pain. No member can enjoy success without everyone experiencing joy. With such closeness, it's not surprising that church members also would be involved in the important process of choosing a career.

George W. Truett was an aspiring young lawyer until the members of his church urged him to enter the ministry. They had observed his life and were certain God had gifted him for the gospel ministry. Truett listened to their counsel and became one of the greatest Baptist pastors of the 20th century.

Likewise, the people of your church will have watched your life and witnessed God's activity in it. When you share job or career opportunities with them, they will be able to pray with you while already knowing many of the spiritual markers of your life. As part of a church family, you will be among young couples, college students, senior adults, youth, children, mature Christians, and new converts. You will know those who have been successful in business and those who have not, those who have struggled with their obedience to God and those who are pillars of faith. You will have access to the prayer warriors of your church who can intercede for you as you make your decision. You will have access to your pastor and other spiritual leaders who can give wise counsel as you seek to determine what God is saying to you. Each will have a unique perspective and experiences in their own walk with God that can help put your decision in focus.

What did God say to you during your study today?

What will you do as a result?

INVESTING YOUR LIFE

> "Peter said to him, 'We have left all we had to follow you!' 'I tell you the truth,' Jesus said to them, 'no one who has left home or wife or brothers or parents or children for the sake of the kingdom of God will fail to receive many times as much in this age and, in the age to come, eternal life" (Luke 18:28-30).

On October 25, 1992, Thomas Alva Edison was awarded a baccalaureate degree from Thomas Edison State College. The unusual thing was not that a man of his brilliance had earned a degree, but that he had done so 61 years after his death! Reese Jenkins, a history professor at Rutgers University, led a group of scholars to put together portfolios demonstrating Edison's learning. Edison's degree was not based on classes he had attended but on the contributions he made to society through his expertise.

Edison's example suggests that the important thing is not the courses taken or the degree earned but the life lived. A college education is not the end but the beginning. The education you obtain is merely a tool God gives you so you can be more effective in His assignment for you. The question at the end of life will not be "What degree did you earn?" but "How did you invest your life for God's glory?"

JOHN AND JUDAS

The disciples John and Judas received the same basic education from Jesus. Both were trained for their calling during the three and a half years spent under Jesus' teaching. The education made no apparent impact on Judas. He left "school" and tragically wasted his life. After John's schooling, he was a changed man. He took the education he received and invested it in eternity. History was forever changed because of the investment John made.

Are you making career choices based on the way God might influence eternity through you? Explain your response.

How do you think your training and career could affect the kingdom of God?

THE CAMBRIDGE SEVEN

In 1885 Britain's attention was seized by seven university graduates who appeared to many to be throwing their lives away. All seven young men came from wealthy families and had received the finest education available. Several were gifted athletes. For example, C. T. Studd was the captain of the Cambridge cricket team and was considered to be one of the finest cricket players in Britain. All seven had every opportunity available to wealthy young men, but each one dedicated himself to mission service in China. They became known as the Cambridge Seven and captivated the interest of Britain by walking away from lives of wealth and high society to spend their lives toiling in humble conditions on the other side of the world.

Many of these men faced strenuous appeals to forget their enterprise and take their place in polite society. However, they chose to follow their calling. Montague Beauchamp worked in China as an evangelist and later as a chaplain in Egypt, Greece, and Russia. He was offered an enormous fortune if he would return to Britain, but he refused. William Cassels served in China until his death. Dixon Hoste spent his life in China and was interred by the Japanese during World War II. Arthur Pohill ministered in China for 43 years. Cecil Pohill labored in China and eventually Tibet. Stanley Smith spent his entire life ministering in China. C. T. Studd served nine years in China before illness forced him home. Upon his return to Britain, he gave away his entire fortune. He later spent six years in India and then 21 years in Africa, where he eventually died. Due in large part to the testimony of these men in Britain and the United States, the Student Missionary Volunteer movement was formed and encouraged many people to go around the world as missionaries.

A biographer of these men concluded his account by saying, "Not one of the Seven, except possibly C. T. Studd, was a genius. Theirs is a story of ordinary men, and thus may be repeated."[2]

The inspirational thing about the Cambridge Seven is that they had everything this world has to offer, but they chose to turn their backs on it to follow Jesus. As a result, only God knows how eternity was altered for good. Until the end of time, people will read of their lives and be encouraged to follow their selfless example.

Notice the promise below that Jesus made to His disciples as they were evaluating the investment they were making with their lives:

> "Peter said to him, 'We have left all we had to follow you!' 'I tell you the truth,' Jesus said to them, 'no one who has left home or wife or brothers or parents or children for the sake of the kingdom of God will fail to receive many times as much in this age and, in the age to come, eternal life' " (Luke 18:28-30).

What did Jesus suggest you might have to give up to follow Him?

Have you had to give up anything in order to obey Jesus' call in your life? What was it?

What does Jesus say the return of your investment will be?

Jesus was not unsympathetic to the price some would have to pay to follow Him. He just knew that the cost of not following Him would be far greater, and the reward for following would greatly surpass any loss. Jesus pointed to important things in people's lives: home, wife, brothers, parents, children. When we served in Canada, we received a number of somber phone calls from those who said they dearly wanted to come and labor with us in pioneer missions, but they could not bring themselves to leave their home state. One young lady of 18 was threatened by her father that he would kill her if she was baptized in our church! She trembled all through her baptism. Upon her return home, she was not harmed, but her suitcase was packed and waiting on the back porch. She had been forced to give up her home and her parents. There will be some hard decisions to make when you consider whether to invest in the temporal or the eternal.

PLACED BY GOD

We spoke recently with a young man who was questioning why God had placed him in his job. It was a good job in the computer field. His responsibility was to relate to the top executives of some of the most prestigious companies in America. He commented that he was not sure how his life was "making an impact for God." I immediately sensed that God was intentionally putting this young man beside some of the most influential men and women in America for a Christian witness.

Many times we've been impressed with how God has strategically placed people in positions that are exactly where He needs one of His servants in order to carry out His redemptive purposes. We have talked with computer experts who rejoiced to find that their skills were desperately needed to assist Christian ministries in their effectiveness. School teachers perceived they were strategically positioned to influence impressionable minds toward Christ. Lawyers found that God was introducing them to some of the most hopeless men and women in society, many of whom were open to the gospel. Agriculturists have realized their particular skills were urgently needed internationally by people who, once they were fed, were ready to hear the gospel. Engineers have seen that through short-term mission opportunities they could revolutionize entire towns and villages physically and spiritually through their skill and knowledge. Businesspeople ascertained that through the material wealth with which God had blessed them, they could support struggling mission churches and other Christian causes.

> MANY TIMES I HAVE BEEN IMPRESSED
> WITH HOW GOD HAS STRATEGICALLY PLACED PEOPLE
> IN POSITIONS THAT ARE EXACTLY WHERE HE NEEDS
> ONE OF HIS SERVANTS IN ORDER TO CARRY OUT
> HIS REDEMPTIVE PURPOSES.

How might God use you in your career choices for His kingdom?

Are you taking God's purposes into account as you prepare yourself for your career? How?

Always look at a career from the perspective of eternity. List ways God might use these professions to build His kingdom.

Nurse:
Businessperson:
Engineer:
Teacher:
Lawyer:
Other:

How can God use the profession you're seeking or are in for His glory?

God can do more with your occupation than you could imagine. A pediatrician, for instance, has numerous opportunities to serve God. She could be an active member of her church. He could minister to parents and children in a Christian manner, demonstrating God's love. Her office could provide Christian literature and music in the waiting room. He might serve in short-term missions in a needy place or use his income to sponsor mission work. Likewise, your profession, placed in the hands of the Lord, could become a powerful instrument for the furthering of God's kingdom.

DOCTORS ON MISSION

We had several medical students in our church. Some of them used their internship to serve on international mission fields and later were active in their churches. One medical graduate teamed with three other young doctors to settle in another part of the country where there was a need not only for a medical practice but also a church. The four partners committed to become the nucleus of a new church and to give their finances to support a pastor.

There are people who assume that unless they are training to serve as a pastor or a missionary they do not have to consider how God might use their lives and occupations for His service. Every occupation is a calling from God. You can settle for the mediocrity of getting the job done and living for the weekend, or you can ask God to consecrate your work and use you to make a significant difference in His kingdom.

List the four ways God speaks to you.

1.

2.

3.

4.

What did God say to you during your study today?

What will you do as a result?

4

RELATIONSHIPS: FOR BETTER OR FOR WORSE

" I tell you the truth, whoever accepts anyone I send accepts me; and whoever accepts me accepts the one who sent me" (John 13:20).

ON JULY 27, 1991, Kevin Brundrett, Stephen West, and Richard Letung went skydiving outside Kitchenor, Ontario. As the trio began their descent, West's and Letung's tandem parachutes became entangled, causing them to flap uselessly in the wind while the two friends plummeted toward the ground. Brundrett maneuvered himself over to them and, rather than pulling his rip cord, vainly attempted to disentangle their parachutes. Brundrett was a photographer and had placed a camera in his helmet so the entire sequence of dramatic events was captured on film. The film shows Brundrett desperately trying to pull up on his two friends' snarled lines to slow their fatal descent. Brundrett's parachute was in perfect working order and he could have pulled his rip cord at any moment to break his fall. But he refused to abandon his friends. All three were killed on impact.[1]

Jesus said, "Greater love has no one than this, that he lay down his life for his friends" (John 15:13). This is Jesus' standard for relationships, whether it is with your spouse, friend, or parent.

FRIENDSHIPS

> " Greater love has no one than this, that he lay down his life for his friends"
> (John 15:13).

Jesus knew the value of friends. The home of Lazarus, Martha, and Mary was a favorite place for Him to visit (Luke 10:38-42; John 11:1-5; 12:1-3). His Heavenly Father gave Him twelve disciples to be His companions (John 17:6-8). Of these, Peter, James, and John became His closest friends. They were with Him during several of the crucial moments in His life (Matthew 17:1-8; 26:36-46; Luke 8:49-56).

Name three of your closest friends and why they are special to you.

Jesus was concerned that believers learn how God intended for them to relate to one another. To this end, He gave a beautiful demonstration of genuine friendship.

Read John 13:1-20; then answer the following questions.

At what point in Jesus' life did He teach this lesson? Why was this time significant?

What lesson was Jesus trying to teach His disciples?

Why do you think Jesus concluded by saying, "Whoever accepts me accepts the one who sent me"?

Would it have been difficult for you to wash the disciples' feet? Why?

The timing of this event is important. It occurred during the Last Supper, the night Jesus would be arrested and condemned to crucifixion. Jesus knew He had little time left. Every word and action in His final hours was critical. At such a climactic moment, Jesus took a significant amount of time to teach them how they should treat one another. This lesson was highly practical. After walking a long distance in sandals on dusty roads, each disciple needed his feet washed. In their culture, feet were considered inherently unclean. So demeaning was it to wash someone's feet that Jewish slaves were not obligated to perform such a degrading task. Without a Gentile servant available, each disciple must have waited awkwardly, wondering what to do. Perhaps Jesus was looking to see if any of His disciples would serve the others. If so, He waited in vain. So Jesus took the washbasin and towel and began washing each disciple's feet, including Judas, who soon would use those feet to run and betray Him. By performing such a menial task, Jesus was teaching that a friend is willing to put the needs of others before his own comfort.

Describe the last time you left your comfort zone in order to meet the need of a friend.

In John 13:20 Jesus taught the disciples a valuable truth. Christ resides by His Spirit in every Christian. When you meet a Christian, you encounter Christ. When you neglect or mistreat a fellow Christian, you are doing so to your Lord. This provides strong motivation for serving others! You are not to evaluate each person's worthiness or question if they should be serving you. It's irrelevant whether they can repay your kindness.

To our amazement we find that many Christians do not know how to be a friend. They are eager to receive but have no idea how to give. We talk with many young adults who complain that they lack close friends. But you have to be a friend to have a friend. We remember one young man who complained that no one called on him socially. No one seemed to care whether he attended student events. He felt rejected and was considering dropping out of his Christian student organization. We examined his situation from another perspective: To whom was he currently ministering? Was he aware of those around him who were in difficult times? How many times had he called others and offered his services? He had not realized that the problem lay with him, and he became determined to concentrate on being a friend.

Many people are ready to share their problems, but far fewer are willing to listen and take a genuine interest in others as Jesus did. As a Christian, you are without excuse for not knowing how to extend friendship. Jesus clearly demonstrated what a true friend is like. A friend looks for needs in others and then meets them to the best of his or her ability. A friend looks for Jesus' activity in the lives of others and then joins God in His work.

Qualities of a Christian Friend

These are the qualities Scripture says ought to be characteristic of a friend.

1. Faithful: Proverbs 17:17; 20:6
2. Honest: Proverbs 3:3-4
3. Good counselor: Proverbs 11:14; 12:15; 15:22; 19:20-21; 24:6; 27:9
4. Demonstrates spiritual fruit: Galatians 5:22-23
5. Wise: Proverbs 13:14, 20
6. Loving: Proverbs 17:17
7. Slow to anger: Proverbs 19:11; 22:24
8. Has integrity: Proverbs 10:9; 11:3; 11:30; 13:3; 20:7
9. Humble: Proverbs 22:4

What kind of friend are you? Rate yourself on the following scale.

I give to others without expecting to receive.
❑ **Always** ❑ **Sometimes** ❑ **Never**

I treat my friends as I would treat Christ.
❏ Always ❏ Sometimes ❏ Never

I feel hurt if people do not minister to me.
❏ Always ❏ Sometimes ❏ Never

I watch for needs I can meet.
❏ Always ❏ Sometimes ❏ Never

I find joy in helping my friends.
❏ Always ❏ Sometimes ❏ Never

I keep a 50-50 relationship with my friends.
❏ Always ❏ Sometimes ❏ Never

I am too busy for friends.
❏ Always ❏ Sometimes ❏ Never

I prefer being by myself.
❏ Always ❏ Sometimes ❏ Never

I consider myself a good friend.
❏ Always ❏ Sometimes ❏ Never

I am a reliable friend.
❏ Always ❏ Sometimes ❏ Never

I am loyal.
❏ Always ❏ Sometimes ❏ Never

How do you measure up as a friend? What things need improvement?

It's said that the way to tell if someone is a leader is by looking to see if anyone is following. Perhaps the way to tell if you are a good friend is to see if you have friends. If you found that you didn't rate well, read John 13 again. Ask God to help you become a friend to others. Allow Christ to love others His way through you.

IRON SHARPENS IRON

Read the wise advice Scripture gives about friendship in Proverbs 27:17.

According to Proverbs, what kind of influence should Christians have on one another? How does this happen?

Why do people need to be sharpened?

The Bible tells us iron sharpens iron. Rub feathers or cotton balls against a dull knife as hard as you want—the blade remains dull. It's the same with friends. There are those people who never challenge you to grow as a Christian. There are others, however, whose lives have a positive influence on you whenever you're around them. The Book of Proverbs consistently urges you to surround yourself with friends who have a positive influence on your life.

One benefits of close relationships is having people who love you enough to hold you accountable. Church leaders and public figures who have fallen into moral failure have had one common denominator: They were accountable to no one. Many Christians today are taking Proverbs 27:17 seriously. They are finding two or three friends and forming an accountability group. These groups meet weekly and:

- Memorize Scripture.
- Tell one another what God said to them in their devotional times the week before.
- Confess areas where they're struggling in obedience to God.
- Hold one another accountable in these areas the following week.

- Pray for one another.
- Challenge each other where they notice danger signals for temptation.

Find friends who want to be absolutely obedient to God and begin meeting with them regularly. It's best to limit the number of people involved so you feel free to share and get to know each other on an intimate level.

How does your love for others compare with Jesus' love for you?

What kind of friend are you? What would you sacrifice for your friends?

List three things you will do to be a better friend. Use Jesus as your model.

What did God say to you during your study today?

What will you do as a result?

DATING RELATIONSHIPS

> "Do you not know that your body is a temple of the Holy Spirit, who is in you, whom you have received from God? You are not your own" (1 Corinthians 6:19).

A 30-year-old pilot stealthily took off in his Cessna 150 airplane at 1:15 a.m. from the Edmonton municipal airport. He then buzzed the Londenderry neighborhood of Edmonton, Alberta, for two hours, insisting on speaking to his former girlfriend by radio. Finally, as his fuel ran out, with his estranged girlfriend still refusing to talk to him, he aimed his plane directly at her home and flew into the front window!

Extreme events like this one demonstrate the terrible pain and confusion prevalent in many relationships between men and women. Divorce, family violence, and infidelity are rampant. In light of this, it's imperative that you seek God's leadership in finding a spouse.

The patterns you establish while dating will affect your marriage. Movies and television have lowered the standards and values in dating relationships to the base maxim of "do what feels good!" You must allow God to establish the guidelines for your dating relationships if you are ever to have a dating life and marriage that pleases Him. What you do while dating reveals your character to God and to others.

The following guidelines may help as you seek to maintain a dating relationship honoring God *and* the person you're dating.

1. PRESENT YOUR MIND TO CHRIST.

Christian dating too often reflects the world's thinking. Because you are a Christian does not mean you are doing "Christian" thinking! Notice what the Scripture below says.

> "Those who live according to the sinful nature have their minds set on what that nature desires; but those who live in accordance with the Spirit have their minds set on what the Spirit desires. The mind of sinful man is death, but the mind controlled by the Spirit is life and peace" (Romans 8:5-6).

What two desires can you set your mind on? What are the results?

Paul warned that concentrating on what the sinful nature desires will lead to death. Society spends billions of dollars encouraging people to satisfy their appetites. Pornography, Hollywood, even prime-time television all portray people as objects to satisfy your lust. If you fill your mind with pornography, soap operas, X-rated books and movies, this will affect your thinking about the opposite sex.

This is why Paul urged in Philippians 4:

> **"Finally, brothers, whatever is true, whatever is noble, whatever is right, whatever is pure, whatever is lovely, whatever is admirable—if anything is excellent or praiseworthy—think about such things" (v. 8).**

Apply this verse to your dating. Are your thoughts about the person you date noble? Admirable? Pure? Acceptable in God's sight? Think about these questions for a few moments right now.

2. PRESENT YOUR BODY TO CHRIST.

God created us male and female. He knew the joy and intimacy that was possible between man and woman in a marriage relationship.

Read 1 Corinthians 6:19.

Henry led a conference some years ago in which God began to convict many young adults about the way they had been relating to each other physically. Men confessed to lust and pornography addiction. Women admitted they had been dressing to tempt and entice men. They realized that their actions were causing others to fall into temptation. They resolved to treat each other in a way that reflected that their bodies were the residence of the Holy Spirit. The way you treat your body reflects how seriously you consider God's habitation in you (Romans 12:1-2).

3. PRESENT YOUR CONVERSATION TO CHRIST.

Read and observe what Jesus said to the religious hypocrites of His day in Matthew 12:34. These are strong words considering He was addressing a group of religious leaders. These pious men purported to be followers of God. In fact, their words were blasphemous! Jesus said that despite our best attempts to conceal it, what's in our hearts will eventually come to light by what we say. Our true self will show through if we talk long enough. It's inevitable. This certainly is true on a date.

You may assume that because you're a Christian your conversation always is holy. Take a few minutes to reflect on the words that come out of your mouth.

While on a date, do you—

❏ **usually talk about yourself?**   ❏ **make fun of others?**

❏ **focus on the negative side of things?**   ❏ **gossip?**

❏ **betray secrets?**   ❏ **criticize others?**

❏ **tell crude jokes and stories?**   ❏ **use profanity?**

Are you pleased with what your conversation reveals about your heart? Why or why not?

How do you honor the person you're with by your conversation?

When you're on a date, do you feel comfortable discussing your relationship with God?

Do the two of you pray together? Do you pray for one another? What do you gain from praying together?

4. PRESENT YOUR DATE TO CHRIST.

Every time you go on a date, you have a four-fold responsibility. You're responsible for the body God gave you; your Christian witness; the reputation of the person you are with; and the name of your family and church. Relationships are a gift from God and are to be enjoyed, but you should approach each one with a sense that there is much at stake.

Notice in this Scripture how Paul said a husband should treat his wife.

> **"Husbands, love your wives, just as Christ loved the church and gave himself up for her to make her holy, cleansing her by the washing with water through the word, and to present her to himself as a radiant church, without stain or wrinkle or any other blemish, but holy and blameless"** (Ephesians 5:25-27).

What is it Christ did for His bride, the church?

Should this apply to dating relationships? Why or why not?

You're to treat your dating relationship the same way Christ loved the church. Christ saw people who were sinful and committed Himself to making them all that God desired. He cleansed the church through His redemptive work on the cross. Now He is preparing the church to be without stain, wrinkle, or blemish, but holy and blameless. This is a beautiful picture of a bridegroom who comes for his bride on their wedding day. Long before this, the bridegroom lovingly helped his future bride become all God intended, so now she would be holy and blameless. The careful stewardship of his bride's life allowed their marriage to begin untarnished.

Does Ephesians 5:25-27 accurately reflect the way you relate to those you date? Why or why not?

5. PRESENT YOUR ACTIVITIES TO CHRIST.

Dating activities are opportunities to develop friendships which, under God's direction, may lead to marriage. These activities hold potential for enjoyment as well as heartache.

Read Galatians 6:7-10. What does it teach us?

Do you see a truth in this Scripture? Record it in the space below.

God says you'll harvest what you plant. If you nurture the spiritual life of the one you're dating and if you act with integrity, then you will enjoy the reward of a healthy relationship. If your dating relationship is based on honoring and serving God, you'll have a solid foundation on which to build a marriage. Some of the young adults in our church went on the most unusual dates! At times their "date" consisted of having a worship service at the downtown rescue mission or a retirement home. Other couples took lonely senior citizens out with them on dates. Relationships were often built on activities in the Christian student organization on campus. God blessed many of these couples, and they are still serving Him together today.

Other couples dropped their involvement in organizations or church. They no longer made time to meet with other Christians. This was a recipe for disaster. God wants your relationships to be a blessing to others and not to be selfishly drawn inward. Couples who spend all their time with each other, not making themselves accountable to other Christians, face a much greater chance of falling into sexual sin.

We've had young adults come to us devastated because they were sexually active and they felt unclean and ashamed. Nowhere does the Bible allow for sex outside of marriage. The word the Bible uses to describe sex between unmarried people is *fornication* (Ephesians 5:3; Colossians 3:5; 1 Thessalonians 4:3). Not only are we to avoid this sin, we should flee from it (1 Corinthians 6:18). If you plant seeds of sexual sin while you're dating, you'll harvest the consequences later: guilt, shame, regret, and possibly an unwanted pregnancy or disease. A relationship based on sex is a poor basis for marriage and will create numerous difficulties for the couple throughout their married life.

Paul offered hope to those facing this kind of temptation. Read what he promised in the Scripture below.

> "No temptation has seized you except what is common to man. And God is faithful; he will not let you be tempted beyond what you can bear. But when you are tempted, he will also provide a way out so that you can stand up under it" (1 Corinthians 10:13).

What does this verse say about temptation?

How does God deliver you from temptation?

How might this be applied to sexual temptation?

Few temptations are as compelling as sexual sin. Even King David, the man after God's own heart, succumbed to it. Paul assures us that even sexual temptation is not powerful enough to overcome you. However, notice how God delivers you—He provides an opportunity to flee from the temptation. The best time for escape is not at the last minute. The moment the Holy Spirit first begins to alert you to danger is the time to flee!

What did God say to you during your study today?

What will you do as a result?

MARRIAGE RELATIONSHIPS

> "The LORD God said, 'It is not good for the man to be alone. I will make
> a helper suitable for him'" (Genesis 2:18).

Some people will do anything to ensure that their marriage gets off to a good start! Holly Holden and Roland Flaig were getting married in Winnipeg, Canada, and, like many young couples, they wanted their wedding day to be memorable. It was! The ceremony took place at center ice between periods of a professional hockey game. The guest list included 12,500 fans, including the premier of the province. Flanking the wedding party was a large blue and white mascot named Benny and two radio person-alities. Nevertheless, they would find that it's not the wedding, no matter how flashy, that determines the success of a marriage, but the biblical guidelines that are followed.

We've encountered marriages filled with great joy and fulfillment. Sadly, we've also known couples whose marriages held deep heartache. Marriage is one of God's greatest gifts. As a young adult, you probably are considering and praying about marriage. You may already be married. Except for your relationship with Christ, no invitation from God has deeper potential for fulfillment than marriage to the right person (Proverbs 31:10-31). At the same time, no relationship holds the possibility for deeper hurt than a poor marriage.

Today's study will look at God's pattern for marriage and choosing a life partner. However, you may be doing this study from the background of divorce; an abusive home; pressure from attitudes and values of the world around you; the horror stories of others; or just an honest fear of marriage. Don't allow the failures of others in marriage to rob you of what God may have in store for you. If your parents didn't model God's ideal for marriage, it's imperative that you seek guidance from God's Word and take your view of marriage from there.

What about marriage worries you?

The Book of Hebrews says, "Marriage should be honored by all" (Hebrews 13:4). Marriage is a good thing, established by God at creation. Notice what Genesis says about the first marriage in Genesis 2:18.

Why did God establish marriage?

How is the wife described here in Genesis?

God first established marriage for companionship. The word *helper* doesn't denote inferiority; it's the same word used in the Old Testament to describe God's relationship with His people. This verse describes the joining of two people so that they're made stronger together than when they were apart. The woman was "suitable" for the man, meaning that no other creature was adequate for the intimate level of relationship God desired for man. Together, husband and wife are able to help each other achieve all that God has planned for them.

If you've experienced divorce or marital strife, how has this affected you? How can you allow God to help you forgive, break the chain, and establish a Christ-centered home?

> PERHAPS THE GREATEST TRAGEDY AMONG YOUNG ADULTS
> IS WHEN THEY REFUSE TO TRUST THAT GOD
> WILL GIVE THEM HIS BEST. SOME PANIC AND MARRY
> SOMEONE THEY KNOW IN THEIR HEART
> IS NOT GOD'S BEST FOR THEM.

FALLING IN LOVE

The best prevention for divorce is to marry wisely. It's important to recognize that you can fall in love with more than one person. God made each of us in His image (Genesis 1:26-28), and each has a God-given purpose. Therefore, many people have the potential to become special to you. We've known young adults who planned to marry someone with whom they were obviously incompatible. Yet when asked why they were getting married, they answered, "We're in love!" This sounds great, but feelings can be deceptive. The obvious question, then, is, "If being in love is not enough on which to base my marriage, what do I use as a standard?" God's Word holds the answer. Consider the following guidelines.

1. TRUST GOD'S PLAN FOR YOUR LIFE.

Read what Jeremiah 29:11 teaches us about God's plan for our lives:

> "'I know the plans I have for you,' declares the LORD, 'plans to prosper you and not to harm you, plans to give you hope and a future.'"

Do you trust God's will for your marriage? Do you believe that God will give you only that which is an expression of His perfect love? This may mean His special assignment is for you to remain single; that could be His expression of love to you. If He wants you to marry later in life, that's what He will lead you to do. The important thing is that however He leads you, that's where you'll find peace and joy, lacking nothing.

Perhaps the greatest tragedy among young adults is when they refuse to trust that God will give them His best. Some panic and marry someone they know in their heart is not God's best for them. As graduation approaches, they may feel pressure to be married. Or they may become depressed if they pass the age at which they always thought they would marry. As more of their friends get married, they may determine to marry also. We've urged many young adults in these situations to trust that God's will is always best for them and never to take matters into their own hands. Waiting sometimes is the hardest form of obedience.

Single but Hopeful!

We came to know a marvelous woman named Evelyn. For many years she faithfully served the Lord as a missionary in India and then in Venezuela. When her mother became elderly, Evelyn returned home to care for her. She joined our church, taught in our Bible college, and befriended many of our young adults. Evelyn had never married, but had committed her life to God's perfect will. Smiling, she often would tease, "I'm single but still hopeful!" After her mother passed away, God introduced Evelyn to a widowed missionary and they were married. Today they enjoy a wonderful ministry sharing the gospel with Sikhs in Canada.

Are you ready to trust God for your marriage partner (see Psalm 84:11)? If not, what's holding you back?

If you're married, how can God enrich and protect your relationship?

2. CULTIVATE YOUR MOST IMPORTANT RELATIONSHIP.

Jesus said, "Seek first his kingdom and his righteousness, and all these things will be given to you as well" (Matthew 6:33). He also instructed, "Do not worry about tomorrow" (Matthew 6:34). Jesus said in Matthew 6:8, "Your Father knows what you need before you ask him." God promised that if you always place Him first, He'll provide for every need in your life. That includes marriage.

3. DETERMINE TO MARRY ONLY A COMMITTED CHRISTIAN.

Few biblical instructions, when ignored, have created more sorrow and pain than Paul's warning: "Do not be yoked together with unbelievers. For what do righteousness and wickedness have in common? Or what fellowship can light have with darkness? What harmony is there between Christ and Belial [the devil]? What does a believer have in common with an unbeliever?" (2 Corinthians 6:14-15). The Bible is absolutely clear; Christians should not marry non-Christians. Paul said Christians and non-Christians are fundamentally different. One is a servant of Christ; the other is an enemy of Christ. One is light, the other darkness. One seeks to put Christ first in everything; the other lives for self. It's an impossible combination.

We've seen much heartache in Christians who married unbelievers. Their hopes, as well as the promises of their unbelieving fiancés, never materialized. As pastors, we had several wonderful Christians who served faithfully in the church; however, they served alone. Their non-Christian partners rarely, if ever, attended church or supported their ministry. Often their spouses would ridicule their faith and refuse to cooperate in raising their children to honor God. One husband even killed his Christian wife in a fit of anger. These people suffered greatly from being yoked with an unbeliever and often would plead tearfully for the church to pray for their husband or wife. Their agony confirmed in our hearts that the most effective way to avoid marrying an unbeliever is not to date them. Remember, you can develop feelings for people if you spend enough time with them. Be careful you don't spend too much time with those God forbids you to marry.

How can you pray for your current or possible future spouse?

SAMSON'S EXAMPLE

Judges 14–16 tells the story of Samson, a young man for whom God had big plans. God blessed Samson with unusual strength. Yet Samson was attracted to a woman named Delilah. Delilah may have had physical beauty, but she didn't revere God or love Samson. By marrying the wrong person, Samson forfeited what God might have done with his life, to say nothing of his own happiness. This story stands as a poignant example of the dangers of marrying an unbeliever. Notice the example of the couple in the Scripture below.

> "In the time of Herod king of Judea there was a priest named Zechariah, who belonged to the priestly division of Abijah; his wife Elizabeth was also a descendant of Aaron. Both of them were upright in the sight of God, observing all the Lord's commandments and regulations blamelessly" (Luke 1:5-6).

What characteristics do you notice about this couple?

Zechariah and Elizabeth were "upright in the sight of God." Can you imagine a marriage relationship in which God saw you and your spouse as upright and blameless in your obedience to Him? No wonder God gave them such an honor. Zechariah and Elizabeth were the parents of John the Baptist. These people were not extraordinary. They simply were people who were deeply committed to God and united to obey His will for their family. What could God do through you and your family? Only He knows! Be absolutely faithful to Him and see what He unfolds for your life!

What character traits does God require for those couples He uses and blesses? Begin praying each day that God will build these qualities into your life and relationships.

What did God say to you during your study today?

What will you do as a result?

FAMILY RELATIONSHIPS

> "I have been reminded of your sincere faith, which first lived in your grand-mother Lois and in your mother Eunice and, I am persuaded, now lives in you also. For this reason I remind you to fan into flame the gift of God, which is in you through the laying on of my hands" (2 Timothy 1:5-6).

I (Henry) had the privilege of being raised by Christian parents who regularly prayed for me and encouraged me to walk closely with God. Considering their influence, it's not surprising that I committed my life to Christ and became a pastor. Several years ago, however, I made an interesting discovery. I was visiting England and Wales for the first time to see the home of my ancestors.

I preached in a church in Wales and discovered there had been four Blackabys who had preached there before me. In the days when the famous Charles Haddon Spurgeon led his Bible college, three of my forefathers were there preparing themselves to be min-isters. God spoke to me: "My work in your family didn't begin with you or your parents. I have been working in your family for much longer than you know. Many of your rela-tives have faithfully served Me, and now it's your turn." God assured me that much of the blessing I enjoyed was because of their faithfulness to God in their day.

Perhaps you've been blessed with a Christian grandmother who prayed for you; an uncle who was a missionary; parents who took you to church. If so, you now have a responsibility to take the baton and run your portion of the race well. Or maybe you're a first-generation Christian. You may not know another Christian in your extended family. God's invitation to you is to begin the Christian heritage in your family, and several gen-erations from now your descendants will look to you as the originator of the good work God has done in your family.

A HERITAGE HONORED

Paul wrote to Timothy about his family heritage. Read what he said in 2 Timothy 1:5-6.

What did Timothy receive from his grandmother and mother?

What was Timothy to do to avoid taking this for granted?

Timothy had a "sincere faith" that Paul recognized as a response to the example of his grandmother and mother. Because of their faithful witness and prayers, Timothy developed his own faith. Paul urged Timothy not to take this Christian heritage for granted, but to build upon the faith that had been passed on to him.

A HERITAGE DISHONORED

A young man became dissatisfied with his life. He came from a good home with parents who loved him. They gave him every opportunity for happiness and success and were, even then, grooming him for the family business. This young man, however, was restless. He felt stifled. Despite his parents' pleading, he took an early inheritance and traveled abroad. There he found some "fast-paced" friends, the kind who lived only for the next party. Because of his wealth, the young man instantly became popular. He gratified all his desires and enjoyed himself. Life seemed better than ever. Then his money ran out, and so did his friends. He looked in vain for a job to support his lavish lifestyle. Driven at last by hunger, he was forced to take a demeaning job at starvation wages. In poverty and shame, his mind was flooded with fond memories of his home and the love he had experienced. He concluded that his home life had to be better than what he was experiencing, and he headed home.

As Jesus told this story in Luke 15:11-32, He said that when the prodigal son returned, his father was watching for him. When he saw his errant son in the distance he was filled with joy and, disregarding dignity or protocol, ran to meet him. Jesus told this story to illustrate the love and forgiveness our Heavenly Father has for us and the joy He experiences when we return to Him.

This same pattern often occurs while in college. We've spoken with many young adults who were raised in Christian homes. Then in college they were swept up in a blatantly immoral environment. Before long, many of the values, beliefs, and practices the students were raised to affirm are discarded for the new lifestyle of living for the moment. How often we've heard young adults weep as they confessed they were prodigal sons or daughters who rejected their Christian heritage, only to discover that what they received in return was emptiness and regret!

The first commandment God gave on relationships was about parents. God says to honor them, showing them respect. Paul noted that this was the only commandment with a "promise" (Ephesians 6:2). The promise is that God will give you a full and meaningful life if you honor your parents. You may feel you cannot honor them because of abuse or neglect you experienced at their hands. This does not cancel the command of God, which He assures brings blessing.

How should you respond to parents who have caused or are causing you pain, suffering, or disappointment?

First, God tells you to forgive. Jesus taught His disciples to pray: "Forgive us our debts, as we also have forgiven our debtors" (Matthew 6:12). The reason to pray this way, Jesus said, is because "if you forgive men when they sin against you, your heavenly Father will also forgive you. But if you do not forgive men their sins, your Father will not forgive your sins" (Matthew 6:14-15).

YOU ARE TO LOVE YOUR PARENTS.
NO GREATER HONOR CAN YOU BESTOW ON YOUR PARENTS
THAN TO LOVE THEM AS GOD LOVES YOU.

According to Matthew 6:14-15, on what basis does God forgive your transgressions against Him?

If you forgive your parents, does this mean you haven't been hurt by them? Explain.

Is being deeply hurt by someone an acceptable excuse for not forgiving them? Why?

Second, you are to love them. No greater honor can you bestow on your parents than to love them as God loves you. How does God love you? Romans 5:8 says, "God demonstrates his own love for us in this: While we were still sinners, Christ died for us."

What are some ways God has expressed His love to you?

Third, be completely obedient to God's will. Ultimately there's no better way to honor your parents than by allowing God to work in and through your life to bring Him glory.

Fourth, live a life of holiness that influences others, including your family. Jesus said you are to be the salt and light of the world (Matthew 5:13-16). You may be the only Christian witness your family ever sees. Because they know you so well, the most difficult people in the world to witness to may be your family. However, your family also will notice the changes in you once you become a Christian. When God saved you, it was His invitation for you to join Him in His redemptive work for your family.

When Karen became a Christian as a college student, she was the only Christian in her family. Her father was a known alcoholic in her home town. When she became a Christian, Karen had a new love and concern for him, and she asked us to pray for him. It wasn't long before her father became a Christian, and he remains a strong witness in his community today. Karen's friend Becky, from the same town, also became a Christian, and Becky's mother attended her baptism. So clear was Becky's testimony that her mother tearfully asked if she could speak with the pastor after the service. She had been seeking God for 28 years. That night she put her faith in Christ and within a week invited Becky's church to lead a Bible study in her home 128 miles away. It did, and a church started there that began reaching out to the town and surrounding area.

What are specific ways you can be salt and light to your relatives?

What challenges do you face in witnessing to your relatives?

What specific changes should you make in the ways you relate to your family?

If there are other Christians in your family, list below the influence they had on you.

List those you're praying for and witnessing to as you seek a Christian heritage.

How can you honor and appreciate someone who provided you with a strong Christian influence? Consider writing that person or people a note today.

What did God say to you during your study today?

What will you do as a result?

BROKEN RELATIONSHIPS

> "If you are offering your gift at the altar and there remember that your brother has something against you, leave your gift there in front of the altar. First go and be reconciled to your brother; then come and offer your gift" (Matthew 5:23-24).

As a young adult, I (Richard) participated in a religious survey in the neighborhood surrounding my church. When I came to a house across the alley from the church, I was greeted by a weathered-looking, middle-aged woman. When I told her what I was doing, she said, "Oh, I used to go to that church. In fact, I'm probably still on the membership roll." She went on to describe how 20 years earlier she and her family had attended the church. Then one day, someone in their Sunday School class made an offhand remark that deeply offended them. They left the church and never returned. When I asked about her family, she gave me a pained look. Her oldest daughter was in prison, and her youngest daughter was in a drug rehabilitation center. Her husband had divorced her several years earlier. She told me she watched some religious programming on television and that was all the "church" she had anymore.

As I walked away from her home that afternoon, I was heavyhearted. Here was a woman who had allowed a broken relationship to keep her and her family out of the church for more than 20 years. As she nursed her hurt feelings, her children grew to disregard the teachings of God for their lives. The mother stood alone and embittered, her family crumbling around her, and she never made the connection that her unwillingness to heed God's instruction on reconciliation had caused enormous heartache in her family. As her family was in shambles, she lived across the street from a group of Christians who could have supported her through her times of crisis.

An unmended relationship can fester until it destroys all it touches. God knows how devastating this can be, so He gives clear instructions for reconciliation. Focus on today's memory verse, Matthew 5, again.

> "If you are offering your gift at the altar and there remember that your brother has something against you, leave your gift there in front of the altar. First go and be reconciled to your brother; then come and offer your gift" (vv. 23-24).

Have you experienced a broken relationship? What experiences often bring that relationship to mind?

What does Jesus say to do about the relationship?

According to this passage, does it matter who is at fault? What steps do you need to take today to reconcile the relationship?

Jesus gave clear instructions for those suffering from broken relationships. The context of Jesus' example is this: you come to church and, in the course of your worship, realize there's someone who has something against you. In this example, it's the other person who's upset with you. It may be something you did that offended them or perhaps something they only thought you did. Regardless of the legitimacy of their concern, the directions are the same. Jesus said "go" and "be reconciled." That is, as a Christian, if you realize someone is angry with you, don't wait for them to come to you. Rather, always take the initiative and go to them. Interestingly, the command is not "try and be reconciled" or "do what you can and hope they get over it" but "Be reconciled!" You take the responsibility to strive for reconciliation and don't give up until you've been reconciled! Christians should never be satisfied as long as they know someone has "something" against them. A broken relationship affects your relationship with God and therefore will cost you dearly, maybe for years.

THE COST OF NOT RECONCILING
IS ALWAYS FAR GREATER
THAN THE COST OF RECONCILING.
RECONCILIATION IS ALWAYS
WORTH IT AND ALWAYS PLEASING TO GOD;
IT SETS YOU FREE!

Do you have any broken relationships right now? With whom?

What has happened in you because of your broken relationship? What has happened to others?

It's important to see how God looks at broken relationships. He wants life's best for you. God opposes anything that robs you of His best.

CHRIST BRINGS RECONCILIATION

Read Romans 5:6-10. Based on this Scripture:

What did Christ do for you?

Who paid the biggest price for your reconciliation, you or God?

How does reconciliation with God bring life?

God took the initiative to be reconciled with you. He committed no offense. He loved you, yet you were an enemy of His. God refused to accept the broken relationship. He didn't wait for you to come to Him; God paid the price for reconciliation. You'll find that often the offended person must pay the higher price to bring reconciliation. The cost of not reconciling is always far greater than the cost of reconciling. Reconciliation is always worth it and always pleasing to God; it sets you free!

What are some serious consequences of your not being reconciled with others?

What's preventing you from taking the initiative to reconcile broken relationships today? Why?

GOD GIVES THE STRENGTH

In her powerful book *The Hiding Place* Corrie Ten Boom told of when she first came face-to-face with a prison guard who had tormented her during her imprisonment in the Ravensbruck concentration camp during the latter days of World War II. As she recalled:

> "It was at a church service in Munich that I saw him, the former S.S. man who stood guard at the shower room door in the processing center at Ravensbruck. ... He came up to me as the church was emptying, beaming and bowing. 'How grateful I am for your message, *Fraulein*.' he said. 'To think that, as you say, He has washed my sins away!' His hand was thrust out to take mine. And I, who had preached so often to the people in Bloemendaal the need to forgive, kept my hand at my side. Even as the angry, vengeful thoughts boiled through me, I saw the sin of them. Jesus Christ had died for this man; was I going to ask for more? *Lord Jesus,* I prayed, *forgive me and help me to forgive him.* ... I felt nothing, not the slightest spark of warmth or charity. ... *Jesus, I cannot forgive him. Give Your forgiveness.* As I took his hand the most incredible thing

happened. From my shoulder along my arm and through my hand, a current seemed to pass from me to him, while into my heart sprang a love for this stranger that almost overwhelmed me. And so I discovered that it is not on our forgiveness any more than on our goodness that the world's healing hinges, but on His. When He tells us to love our enemies, He gives, along with the command, the love itself."[2]

How was Corrie able to forgive her former guard?

How could this type of forgiveness happen in your life?

What did God say to you during your study today?

What will you do as a result?

5

CRISES: YOUR MOMENTS OF DECISION

"We know that in all things God works for the good of those who love him, who have been called according to his purpose" (Romans 8:28).

I (HENRY) LISTENED TO AN AFRICAN-AMERICAN SINGER capture the hearts of hundreds of people as he sang gospel songs in 1987 at the World's Fair in Vancouver. Earnest was a happy man with a tremendous baritone voice. He told me his story. He grew up "on the wrong side of the tracks" in Alabama. One day, in the midst of poverty and hardship, he heard a gospel singer on television. He prayed, "Lord, if you help me to sing, I'll give You my voice to serve You!" He began winning first place in music contests at school. He majored in voice in college. At his graduation recital, a Christian opera singer from the Metropolitan Opera in New York City approached him and asked, "Would you audition for the opera? You are certain to make it!" Earnest went out on a hill overlooking the city to think and pray. There God reminded him, "Earnest, as a boy of 5 years old, you asked Me to help you sing. You said if I did you would give Me your voice. I've done My part. Will you do yours?" Earnest was filled with emotion as he remembered his vow to God. He bowed his head and gave his life to God to sing gospel music wherever God asked. In the midst of hardship, he had decided to put his life entirely into God's hands. He has never gone back on his word and on the day I heard him, he was moving hundreds to tears as he sang for God at the World's Fair in Canada.

A crisis is a challenge but also an opportunity for the Christian. We're tempted during crises to surrender to the world's viewpoint. During such difficult times we endure the loss of friends, ambitions, or possessions and are often discouraged. From a human perspective, crisis means loss. But God plans that we benefit from every trial we face. Examine some benefits of facing a crisis.

CRISES POINT TO GOD'S UNWAVERING LOVE

> "This is how we know what love is: Jesus Christ laid down his life for us"
> (1 John 3:16).

Once you become a young adult, you face some life-changing decisions. Now is the time to prepare yourself for the crises that are certain to come. Many people immediately blame God for every hardship in their lives. They may ask, "Why did God do this to me? If God is so powerful, why didn't He prevent this tragedy?" The way you respond to a crisis can dramatically affect the rest of your life. What you do in times of distress reveals what you believe about God. Unless you clearly understand God's nature, you won't be able to respond properly in times of trial.

Compare 1 John 3:16 above with the Scripture below. Then note what God is like.

> "So we know and rely on the love God has for us. God is love. Whoever
> lives in love lives in God, and God in him" (1 John 4:16).

What one word describes the nature of God to you?

How does God demonstrate His love for you?

GOD'S LOVE IN THE MIDST OF CRISIS

Richard and Lisa were married the summer after they graduated from college and then traveled 1,500 miles to attend seminary. Richard sensed God leading him to be a pastor and knew God wanted him to get a seminary education. As he neared the completion of his master of divinity degree, Richard knew God was inviting him to enter the PhD program. They had already spent three years at seminary and were eager to serve in a church in Canada. Yet they were obedient to God's instructions to stay, and Richard began doctoral studies that fall.

During the first semester of the PhD program, a deluge of crises almost overwhelmed them. Lisa's father suffered a massive heart attack and clung to life for three weeks before dying. In addition to their grief, Richard and Lisa faced financial hardship from work missed, and Richard was far behind in the demanding doctoral program. One month later, Lisa's mother was diagnosed with cancer, a disease that would take her life. The following month, bad news came again, this time about Richard's 16-year-old sister, Carrie. She too had been diagnosed with cancer and would undergo extensive chemotherapy treatments.

In that fall semester they were hit by one tragedy after another. They had been obedient to God. Why was He allowing this to happen? In the following months God did an amazing work in their lives. He made His love, presence, and peace known to them in a deeper way than they had ever experienced. Later, they encouraged many others who were suffering in similar ways. Richard was eventually called as president of the Canadian Southern Baptist Seminary. During the first semester Lisa was asked to speak to the wives of the seminary students. She told them of her own pilgrimage as a student's wife and of the difficulties she had experienced. She shared how the grace of God had sustained her. Many of the women were deeply moved and said, "It means so much to us that you know what we're going through!" In that moment, God affirmed, once more, why He allowed them to endure such suffering. Not only did God want them to experience His peace and comfort, He was also preparing them to minister to seminary students, many of whom would face similar difficulties. God took their loss and brought good from it.

Have you ever tried to be obedient to God, only to face hardships? What happened?

What good did God bring out of the challenges you faced? Did you allow God to work in His timing or take matters into your own hands? Explain.

Should Christians have to face hardships? Why or why not?

God's nature is perfect love. God would have to go against His character to give you less than His best. Settle this point decisively in your mind. God perfectly revealed His love when Jesus died on the cross for your sin even while you were His enemy (John 3:16; Romans 5:5-11). If you ever begin to wonder if God loves you, take a look at the cross. The cross has become a cherished symbol to Christians of the incredible love of God.

GOD'S PROMISES

To experience victory in spite of difficult circumstances, you must believe that God will do all He promises. Second Corinthians 1:20 says, "No matter how many promises God has made, they are 'Yes' in Christ." If you are a Christian, God has made many promises to you. If you ask for any of these, God's answer is always yes!

In the Scripture below, notice what God is ready to give if you're willing to receive. He will express His promises experientially in your life.

> "My God will meet all your needs according to his glorious riches in Christ Jesus" (Philippians 4:19).

> "I tell you the truth, if you have faith as small as a mustard seed, you can say to this mountain, 'Move from here to there' and it will move. Nothing will be impossible for you" (Matthew 17:20).

> "If any of you lacks wisdom, he should ask God, who gives generously to all without finding fault, and it will be given to him" (James 1:5).

Using one sentence for each, summarize the promise God makes to you.

Philippians 4:19

Matthew 17:20

James 1:5

How could God do these things in your situation?

How are you experiencing these promises right now?

Horatio G. Spafford was a devout Presbyterian businessman in Chicago. He enjoyed a close relationship with D. L. Moody and other Christian leaders. During the Chicago fire of 1871, Spafford lost a fortune in real estate. Just before this he had suffered the tragic loss of his only son. Seeking some rest and wanting to assist D. L. Moody in his evangelistic campaigns in Great Britain, Spafford booked passage aboard the Ville du Havre for Europe. A last-minute business development detained him, so his wife set sail with their four daughters with the assurance that Horatio would soon follow. On November 22 the ship collided with the Lochearn, an English ship, and sank in 12 minutes. All four Spafford children drowned. Several days later when the survivors reached Cardiff, Wales, Mrs. Spafford wired her husband, "Saved alone." Spafford took the next ship, and as he sailed past the spot where his children had died, God comforted him in a way he had never before experienced. In the midst of his loss, God poured out love on him, reminding him of the eternal joy that had been granted to his children. Spafford was inspired to write a poem that later became a hymn, "It Is Well with My Soul." Reflect on two of the poem's stanzas:

> When peace, like a river attendeth my way,
> When sorrows like sea billows roll;
> Whatever my lot, Thou hast taught me to say,
> It is well, it is well with my soul.
> Tho' Satan should buffet, tho' trials should come,
> Let this blest assurance control,
> That Christ has regarded my helpless estate
> And hath shed His own blood for my soul.

This song has inspired and encouraged thousands and is still sung today around the world.[1]

If you're going through a difficult time, how can you allow God to redeem your crises for His glory?

How are you preparing for the crises you will inevitably face?

Four Reasons to Trust God
Four truths that affect the way I view God in the midst of crises are:

1. God is love: He always gives what is best for me.
2. God is all-knowing: His Word for my life is always right.
3. God is all-powerful: He will always meet my need.
4. God never changes: I can trust Him in every circumstance.

Do you know God this way? Explain.

Which one of these truths do you struggle to believe? Why?

On a separate sheet of paper, write the four truths about God from memory.

What did God say to you during your study today?

What will you do as a result?

CRISES PROMOTE GAINING LIFE BY LOSING IT

> "I tell you the truth, unless a kernel of wheat falls to the ground and dies, it remains only a single seed. But if it dies, it produces many seeds. The man who loves his life will lose it, while the man who hates his life in this world will keep it for eternal life" (John 12:24-25).

Dr. Joseph Tson was the pastor of Second Baptist Church, Oradea, Romania, during the years of intense communist oppression. On several occasions he was arrested and subjected to long periods of brutal interrogation. During an interrogation in Ploiesti, he was threatened with death if he did not cooperate with the authorities. Joseph replied, "Your supreme weapon is killing. My supreme weapon is dying." He told his captors that his sermons had been recorded on cassette tapes and that he had written tracts to encourage his fellow Christians. He noted that if he were to be executed, people would know he truly believed what he had said and had been willing to die for his beliefs. Thus they would be far more interested in hearing what he had preached. Joseph concluded that the best thing that could happen to him and his message would be his execution!

His captors decided not to execute him, as that would defeat their purpose! Joseph recounted later, "I remember how for many years I had been afraid of dying. Because I wanted badly to live, I wasted my life in inactivity. But now that I had placed my life on the altar and decided I was ready to die for the gospel, they were telling me they would not kill me! As long as I tried to save my life, I was losing it. Now that I was willing to lose it, I found it."[2]

When Jesus guided His disciples to experience God, His teaching often ran contrary to the world's.

Look carefully at His profound words in John 12:24-25.

How do you save your life?

How do you lose your life?

How did Jesus illustrate this principle?

Are you trying to save your life, or have you given it to Christ?

The world teaches that you should always strive to save yourself. It says to never place yourself in a situation where you might be hurt; don't give yourself away to others, but seek all the affirmation and pleasures you can. Our society encourages you to affirm self. Jesus said to deny self. Popular psychology says that man's greatest problem today is low self-esteem. Jesus cautions that your problem is you think too much of yourself.

If you're living with the attitude of saving your life, then you'll be constantly disappointed. For example, if you believe a Christian should not experience pain, your life will be in constant turmoil because this world has suffering.

If you think God wants to give you all of the material desires of your heart, then losing your job will be disastrous! If your focus is on this world and you think God owes you and your family a long and healthy life, then when illness and death come, you will be devastated. Many of our crises come because we assume things that aren't true.

> THE WORLD TEACHES THAT YOU SHOULD ALWAYS STRIVE
> TO "SAVE" YOURSELF. IT SAYS TO NEVER PLACE YOURSELF
> IN A SITUATION WHERE YOU MIGHT BE HURT;
> DON'T GIVE YOURSELF TO OTHERS, BUT SEEK
> ALL THE AFFIRMATION AND PLEASURES YOU CAN.

What assumptions might be influencing your life?

A MATTER OF TRUST

Tammy, a young nursing student in my (Henry's) church, faced a critical point in her life. She was nearing graduation and had no prospect of marriage. All her life she had desired and planned for marriage. Now time seemed to be racing by and God had not answered her earnest prayers for a husband. Her dreams seemed to be crumbling when she came to me for counsel. I shared Romans 8:32, which says, "He who did not spare his own Son, but gave him up for us all—how will he not also, along with him, graciously give us all things?" I told her I would pray for her. But I challenged her, "If God, in His infinite wisdom and perfect love, should decide it's best for you not to marry, could you trust Him and accept this?" Tammy was a faithful Christian, but getting married was very important to her. Ultimately, she decided she could trust God completely with her future, whether she was married or single. She later shared with me that God had given her peace and contentment regardless of her marital status.

She lost her life to God, releasing even her most treasured hope. Soon after that, a Christian young man joined our church. I performed their wedding, and they now have two beautiful children. By losing her life to God, Tammy saved it.

THE COST OF OBEDIENCE
There is no such thing as Christianity without cost.

Read Philippians 2:5-11. How would you describe Jesus' attitude?

What did Jesus give up in order to obey His Father?

What was the result of Jesus' suffering?

How can you follow Jesus' example?

How would your life change if you adopted the mind of Christ?

Consider the trials Jesus endured. His home had been heaven. Yet Jesus did not regard this position as a right. He did not have the attitude that God the Father owed this to Him. When God's will was for His Son to give up everything, Jesus accepted the assignment. He was obedient, even to the point of an excruciating and humiliating death. No mathematician could calculate the distance from the right hand of God to the cross. None of us will ever experience such an extreme change in circumstance. What was the result of Jesus' obedience in crisis? His Heavenly Father exalted Him to the highest place and He will be worshiped forever. His life will bring salvation to billions and His obedience will bring glory to the Father like no other act in all eternity.

Which of the following situations could you entrust to God? Circle them.

Loss of job	Parents' divorce
An impossible task	A sibling addicted to drugs
Bankruptcy	Betrayal from someone you trusted
Death of a loved one	Flunking out of college
Chronic health problems	Abuse
Other: _____	

THE COST OF DISCIPLESHIP

Dietrich Bonhoeffer was an outstanding young pastor and theologian in Germany. He had a brilliant mind and was attaining international prominence when Adolf Hitler came to power. In 1937 he wrote *The Cost of Discipleship,* which challenged Christians not to settle for a superficial religion but to strive for absolute loyalty and obedience to Christ. Bonhoeffer was deeply disturbed by what Hitler was doing in Germany and strenuously opposed it. This caused him to lose his church and to be ostracized by many of Germany's religious and political leaders. As pressures mounted, friends in the United States enticed him to come and deliver a series of lectures in order to get him out of Germany before the war began. Soon, however, Bonhoeffer felt compelled to return to his homeland.

After his return he became involved in rescuing Jewish people and eventually was implicated in a plot to assassinate Hitler. While imprisoned, he ministered to fellow prisoners, many on death row, through his prayers, exhortation, and personal example of trust in God. One Sunday as he led a worship service for his companions, Gestapo guards came and took Bonhoeffer away. His last words to those in the service were "This is the end, for me, the beginning of life." The next morning, on April 9, 1945, Bonhoeffer was hanged at the execution shed at the Flossenburg concentration camp, only three weeks before Hitler committed suicide. The doctor who witnessed his execution declared, "In the almost 50 years that I have worked as a doctor, I have hardly ever seen a man die so entirely submissive to the will of God." After the war's end, Bonhoeffer's writings were widely distributed and gained a more serious reading in light of his devotion and martyrdom. Books such as *The Cost of Discipleship* have challenged countless Christians around the world.[3]

What do you need to submit so that you're entirely committed to Christ?

Notice the example of Jesus in the Scripture below.

> "To this you were called, because Christ suffered for you, leaving you an example, that you should follow in his steps. 'He committed no sin, and no deceit was found in his mouth.' When they hurled their insults at him, he did not retaliate; when he suffered, he made no threats. Instead, he entrusted himself to him who judges justly. He himself bore our sins in his body on the tree, so that we might die to sins and live for righteousness; by his wounds you have been healed" (1 Peter 2:21-24).

To what have Christians been called?

List the trials Jesus endured.

What was the result of Jesus' obedience to His Father?

God's primary concern is not that we live a trial-free life. If this were so, He would take us to heaven immediately upon conversion. Rather, He desires to use us to bring sinful humanity to Himself. For this reason He leaves us in an imperfect world, where we are not immune to suffering. It's like a doctor who works on the front lines of a battlefield.

The wounded and dying need him there, but this puts him in danger. Likewise, we live in a spiritual battlefield where good people suffer.

Have you experienced the cost of following Jesus? How?

What might it cost you for God to bring redemption to your friends? Your workplace? Your children? The world?

What might it cost you to not be obedient to what God is telling you?

FACING THE FLAME

One of our favorite Old Testament stories is that of Shadrach, Meshach, and Abednego. These men lived in a pagan society that worshiped idols. When a law was issued that every person must worship an idol, these three refused, despite enormous pressure.

Carefully read their bold statement of faith to the king who threatened to throw them to their deaths in a flaming furnace (Daniel 3:16-18).

Was their faith based on God's delivering them from their crisis? How do you know?

Read Daniel 3:19-28. What was the outcome of their faithfulness?

What an incredible act of faith! These young men were faithful to God even when those around them were not. What was the reward for their faithfulness? A death threat! But notice their response. They said, we know God could deliver us from this crisis, but whether or not He does makes no difference to us. Our faithfulness to God is not based on whether He protects us from hardship. It is based on the fact that we know He is God and we know He loves us.

Write a prayer in the space below, releasing your life to God, giving up any rights you've been clinging to.

Are you trying to serve God on your terms or have you completely released your life to Him? What's the evidence of this?

What areas of your life do you still need to release to God?

What did God say to you during your study today?

What will you do as a result?

CRISES PROVE THE SINCERITY OF FAITH

> "In this you greatly rejoice, though now for a little while you may have had
> to suffer grief in all kinds of trials. These have come so that your faith—
> of greater worth than gold, which perishes even though refined by fire—
> may be proved genuine and may result in praise, glory and honor when
> Jesus Christ is revealed" (1 Peter 1:6-7).

For the record, 5-year-old Julius Rosenberg is not afraid of bears. Of course, grandiose pronouncements by young children are generally taken with a grain of salt. But on Sunday, September 20, 1992, Julius discovered he really wasn't afraid! He was on the edge of a dock at his family's cottage at West Hawk Lake with his 3-year-old sister, Barbara, when a black bear approached them. The children jumped into the water, but the bear followed them, catching Barbara's life jacket in its mouth. Julius turned and tugged on his sister until the bear released its grip. Julius then stared down the bear, even giving it a fierce growl! The children fled into their cottage, where Julius shouted "A bear bit Barbie, Mommy! The bear bit Barbie!" Their mother saw the bear coming and frantically closed the doors behind the fleeing children to prevent the hungry bear from entering the cottage. No one who knew Julius would have imagined him staring down a hungry bear. But a crisis dramatically confirmed his belief. Julius was not afraid of bears! Crises bring the opportunity to prove what you believe about God.

Notice in Luke 8 what a storm at sea demonstrated about the disciples' faith:

> "One day Jesus said to his disciples, 'Let's go over to the other side of the
> lake.' So they got into a boat and set out. As they sailed, he fell asleep.
> A squall came down on the lake, so that the boat was being swamped,
> and they were in great danger. The disciples went and woke him, saying,
> 'Master, Master, we're going to drown!' He got up and rebuked the wind
> and the raging waters; the storm subsided, and all was calm. 'Where is
> your faith?' he asked his disciples. In fear and amazement they asked one
> another, 'Who is this? He commands even the winds and the water, and
> they obey him'" (vv. 22-25).

With Jesus present, were the disciples really perishing? Explain your answer.

What did they learn about Jesus because of this crisis? How did the adversity make them stronger disciples?

Are you facing a crisis? What pressure is it bringing to bear?

Have you turned to Jesus? What have you learned about Him?

Until recently you may have lived a sheltered life. Perhaps your parents carried the load for you in difficult times. But now you may be exposed to things you've never encountered. You're beginning a stage of life where crises can become more frequent and severe. Are you prepared for them when they come? How will you respond?

FACING DEATH

The doctor approached me (Henry) and said, "Mr. Blackaby, your wife is critically ill. We will have to do immediate surgery. It's serious enough that we may not be able to save her." When they took her away to the operating room, I was left alone with God. The pressure of that moment led me quickly to my relationship with God. We had five children; our daughter was only a few months old. Would God intervene? If He did, how would my family and I live the rest of our lives? Casually? Intensely? This crisis led me to a stronger, more focused relationship with God and His purpose for me and my family. I have sought to live with this intensity ever since. We've experienced so much of the goodness and faithfulness of God in the ensuing years!

Read what Jesus said in Matthew 11:28-30.

Who does Jesus invite to come to Him?

What does Jesus do when you go to Him in your crises?

Jesus encourages His followers to turn to Him when hard times hit. He's not disinterested, letting you work out your problems for yourself. He's not powerless, unable to do anything for you. He's not out of touch, unable to understand what you're going through. He's "gentle and humble," and He's able to bring rest to your soul. He may not always change your circumstance, but He will bring a peace to your heart even in the midst of the most difficult situations if you will trust Him.

BITTER OR BETTER?

Bob was extremely bitter. His father had been an abusive alcoholic. As a young boy, Bob would cry himself to sleep praying that God would change his father. Now as a young man, he came to me (Henry) and said, "My father died an alcoholic." I heard the bitterness in his voice. He had determined that he would have nothing more to do with God. His life reflected that decision. Yet it was obvious that he desperately longed for the love and peace of God. I shared with Bob that God loved his father even more than he did. If God is true to His description in the Bible, He would have been reaching out to Bob's father day after day, urging him to turn from his alcoholism and to let Him change his life. We read passages of Scripture where God urged people to turn to Him and receive healing. Now it was Bob's turn. Would he allow God to heal his brokenness?

Do you have bitterness in your life? How can God heal you?

PAUL'S SUFFERINGS

Read 2 Corinthians 4:7-11 and 11:23-28 and list a few things Paul endured during his Christian life.

How do Paul's sufferings compare with yours?

If Paul underwent such suffering, why do you think he continued to serve God faithfully?

Few people have endured the hardships Paul did. His biography reads like a litany of everything that can possibly go wrong in a Christian's life! Yet this is the same person who wrote Romans.

> "Who shall separate us from the love of Christ? Shall trouble or hardship or persecution or famine or nakedness or danger or sword? No, in all these things we are more than conquerors through him who loved us. For I am convinced that neither death nor life, neither angels nor demons, neither the present nor the future, nor any powers, neither height nor depth, nor anything else in all creation, will be able to separate us from the love of God that is in Christ Jesus our Lord" (Romans 8:35,37-39).

What do these verses say about Paul's confidence that God could give him victory in every circumstance?

Circle the things Paul said could never separate us from the love of God. What fueled Paul's confidence?

Paul was convinced God could bring victory in every circumstance. Paul had experienced enough hardships to know what he was talking about. Yet Paul's confidence was not in the expectation that if he prayed, God would remove his difficulties. Even Jesus did not have His "cup" of suffering taken from Him in the garden of Gethsemane (Luke 22:41-44). Instead, Paul firmly trusted that nothing could ever separate him from the love of God. As long as Paul was experiencing the presence of Christ in his life, he could boldly face the most devastating situations.

HELEN KELLER

The story of Helen Keller is a testimony to the faithfulness of God. Helen grew up unable to hear or speak or see. God brought a teacher, Mrs. Armstrong, to help her. With great difficulty Helen began to turn to God. Because of her unique limitations she came to know God in ways most people never do. As an adult she was able to encourage thousands of hurting people to find assurance and comfort in a relationship with God. Toward the end of her life she was asked: "If you could live your life over again, would you want it to be any different?" Her answer was no. Through her crises she had come to know God so intimately, to experience His love so deeply, and to "see" God so clearly that she would never trade her relationship with Him for anything!

Crises will make you bitter or better. If you release your life to God and accept His will for you as an expression of His perfect love, then God will take you to a depth of relationship with Him that you could not otherwise have experienced.

Briefly describe a crisis one of your friends is enduring.

What might God be inviting you to do to minister to that person?

What did God say to you during your study today?

What will you do as a result?

CRISES PREPARE US FOR GREATER ASSIGNMENTS

> "Consider it pure joy, my brothers, whenever you face trials of many kinds, because you know that the testing of your faith develops perseverance. Perseverance must finish its work so that you may be mature and complete, not lacking anything. Blessed is the man who perseveres under trial, because when he has stood the test, he will receive the crown of life that God has promised to those who love him" (James 1:2-4,12).

Roy Whetstine was a gemologist from Texas. In 1986 he visited a gem and mineral bazaar in Tucson, Arizona. There he spotted an egg-sized violet and blue rock in a Tupperware container, priced at $15. Whetstine offered the owner $10, and the rock was his. He suspected, however, that there was more to this rock than the vendor realized. After months of appraising it, he determined that the rock actually was a 1,905 carat star sapphire with an estimated uncut value of $2.28 million! One man's junk is another man's treasure. The rock had not changed. The difference was in the eye of the beholder. Likewise, crises can be seen in different ways. Some view them as negative, to be avoided at all costs. Others regard them as opportunities for personal and spiritual growth.

There's no greater challenge than a God-sized assignment. That is, any task God gives you that only He is capable of carrying out. Such assignments not only reveal your character, but also help to develop it.

Would you like a God-sized assignment? Are you sure? God-sized tasks are costly. Jesus paid an incredible price to obey His Father. God does not give big assignments to little characters. He looks for someone with a big character and matches His assignment to them. Jesus' mission involved suffering. Carefully read Hebrews 5:

> "During the days of Jesus' life on earth, he offered up prayers and petitions with loud cries and tears to the one who could save him from death, and he was heard because of his reverent submission. Although he was a son, he learned obedience from what he suffered and, once made perfect, he became the source of eternal salvation for all who obey him" (vv. 7-9).

How did Jesus pray to His Father?

Why did God allow Jesus to suffer?

What's an aspect of your character that might be perfected through suffering?

Are you willing to "pay any price" for God to use you mightily in His kingdom? What if that price involves great suffering? Think about and list evidence in your life that reflects this commitment.

Scripture says Jesus prayed with loud cries and tears to His Father, who had the power to save Him from death. God heard Him but allowed Him to suffer. In ways too profound for us to comprehend, Jesus was perfected through His suffering. The word *perfect* also means "complete." For reasons known only to God, Jesus had to suffer if He was to be the Redeemer of humankind. The Son of God already had demonstrated perfect obedience by leaving heaven and walking on the earth without sin, and now He was obedient even when it meant death on a cross.

The perfecting process was painful, but the assignment was enormous!

Who in your circle of family and friends needs salvation? What kind of person would you need to be for God to save them through your influence?

What attitudes, habits, or beliefs does God have to perfect before He can use you?

What matters to God when involving people in His work is character. One way God develops character is through suffering. James encouraged us.

Read James 1:2-4,12 again.

How does James say we should view our trials?

What types of suffering was James referencing?

What can result from our going through trials?

This counsel from James directly contradicts what we naturally would think. We tend to think that only a masochist would experience joy in trials. Yet James says it can be done! In fact, he said to consider it pure joy, that is, joy without any reservation or qualification. Why? Because the tests we go through make us learn perseverance. If you learn to persevere as a Christian, you will become complete and mature, lacking nothing for this life. Ultimately your perseverance will earn you a reward in heaven. These are good reasons for welcoming various trials.

DIFFICULT ASSIGNMENTS

One of the things I (Henry) enjoy most about my work is the opportunity to travel to mission fields around the world to encourage international missionaries. Inevitably I come away challenged by their lives. I met some fine missionary families in the Ukraine where the Chernobyl nuclear power plant disaster occurred, spreading deadly radiation over the land. This catastrophe has been linked to more than 4,300 deaths and has affected more than 3.5 million people. The missionaries serving in that area knew the water they drank and the food they ate was quite likely contaminated by radiation. Yet they also knew that someone had to go and share the gospel with the people who faced this danger daily. The missionary families recognized that God's assignment for them was difficult, and might involve suffering, but they stayed to encourage the people and glorify God.

I met with missionaries serving in war-torn countries in Africa. Many were in mortal danger. With a heavy heart I watched these dedicated people prepare to enter rebel-infested areas where missionaries had already been murdered. God has an assignment for every Christian. Not all will be called as international missionaries. Not all will be called to endure suffering to the same degree. Yet every call of God involves a cross (Matthew 16:24). You cannot follow Christ without taking up your cross. When you face suffering and hardship, will your character and relationship to Christ be of such quality that He can entrust you with His assignment?

SAUL AND DAVID

There is a fascinating contrast between the first two kings of Israel. Saul was the first king. Notice his background in 1 Samuel 9:1-2.

Saul was a strong and handsome man from a respected family. From the outward perspective, Saul seemed like the perfect choice for king. Yet, his reign was disastrous. He became jealous of anyone who received more praise than he did (1 Samuel 18:6-9, 28-29). Saul had a violent temper and was prone to fits of anger (1 Samuel 18:10-12). He became so bitter that he betrayed those who had saved his life and murdered innocent priests who displeased him (1 Samuel 22; 26). Saul grew so conceited that he presumed he could perform the role of priest and blatantly disobeyed a word from God (1 Samuel 15). Saul's life ended in defeat, failure, utter humiliation, and suicide.

David, however, had a different beginning. As a youth he fought lions and bears to defend his father's sheep (1 Samuel 17:37). David's first public assignment from God was to face the terrible giant, Goliath (1 Samuel 17:41-49). David's life was filled with hardship as a young adult. He was in constant danger with many attempts on his life; his wife grew to despise him for his devotion to God (2 Samuel 6:20); his closest friend was separated from him and eventually killed (1 Samuel 20:41-42); many of his good friends and spiritual advisers died (1 Samuel 22:11-19); his wife and possessions were stolen from him (1 Samuel 30:1-6); he lived in caves and even had to feign insanity in order to survive (1 Samuel 21:13). David lived with the frustration of knowing that God wanted him to be king, yet having to wait for years while watching the incompetent King Saul tear the country apart.

Whereas Saul had a relatively easy road toward the monarchy, he did not have the character to flourish in that exalted position. David, however, faced incredible adversity in his spiritual pilgrimage. Yet when he became king, he governed as the greatest monarch ever to rule in Israel. David ruled with compassion and fairness, and when he sinned, unlike Saul, he was sincerely humbled and penitent. He didn't exalt himself, but God. He didn't rule with an iron fist like Saul. God had refined his character so that he would be fit for a significant assignment.

> FOR GOD TO ACCOMPLISH A DIFFICULT WORK,
> HE SOMETIMES REQUIRES SUFFERING.
> AS IT WAS NECESSARY FOR HIS SON TO SUFFER,
> SO AT TIMES IT'S NECESSARY FOR US
> TO SUFFER AS WELL.

How can knowing God is strengthening your faith and character change how you look at your current circumstances?

How is God changing your faith in Him and your character through what you're enduring?

For God to accomplish a difficult work, He sometimes requires suffering. As it was necessary for His Son to suffer, so at times it's necessary for us to suffer as well. Paul declared, "I want to know Christ and the power of his resurrection and the fellowship of sharing in his sufferings, becoming like him in his death" (Philippians 3:10).

What did God say to you during your study today?

What will you do as a result?

DAY 5

MAKING ADJUSTMENTS TO GOD WHEN LIFE LOOKS DARK

> "I sought the LORD, and he answered me; he delivered me from all my
> fears" (Psalm 34:4).

Corrie Ten Boom, in her book *The Hiding Place,* tells the amazing story of when she and her sister Betsie were transferred to the notorious Ravensbruck concentration camp during World War II. As the sisters attempted to go to sleep their first night in Barracks 28, they were repeatedly bitten by fleas. When Betsie prayed and thanked God for their accommodations, including the fleas, Corrie thought she had gone too far! "Betsie, there's no way even God can make me thankful for a flea,"Corrie said. Yet as they adjusted to their life in that horrible death camp, they noticed a strange thing happening. Despite the usual thoroughness of their German prison guards, the Bible they had smuggled in to the barracks was never discovered. Each night the two Christian sisters would read the Bible aloud. The readings were then translated by the prisoners into all the European languages represented in the camp. More and more women listened until eventually the entire barracks of broken and fearful women were clinging desperately to every word. Still, the guards did not find their Bible or intervene in their meetings.

One day the sisters discovered the reason the prison guards had not entered their quarters. The fleas! The guards didn't want to become infested with them, so they neglected to search the barracks. Those tiny creatures of God were actually guarding these women from the mighty German army![4]

God had a difficult assignment. Those abused and discouraged women desperately needed to hear His message of hope and peace, and He needed messengers who would be willing to endure severe deprivation. In the midst of their crisis, Corrie and Betsie had to make enormous adjustments in their lives, but the result was that salvation and hope came to many who were only moments from death.

Crises create moments of decision that affect the rest of your life. God is always present in those dark moments, ready to teach you in the way that leads to life (Matthew 7:13-14). In David's darkest moments he turned to God for strength and help.

Notice what he said in Psalm 34:

"I sought the Lord, and he answered me; he delivered me from all my fears. Those who look to him are radiant; their faces are never covered with shame. This poor man called, and the Lord heard him; he saved him out of all his troubles. The angel of the Lord encamps around those who fear him, and he delivers them. Taste and see that the Lord is good; blessed is the man who takes refuge in him. Fear the Lord, you his saints, for those who fear him lack nothing. The lions may grow weak and hungry, but those who seek the Lord lack no good thing" (vv. 4-10).

What did David do in his time of distress?

How did God respond?

How do you think this affected the way David worshiped and served God?

How does David's experience encourage you?

CARRIE'S CANCER

God gave Marilynn and me (Henry) four wonderful boys. Our youngest child is our daughter, Carrie. She added so much joy to our home. She filled our home with the music of her singing and piano playing. She cheered for her brothers in hockey. Then, when she was 16, the doctors diagnosed her with an advanced case of cancer. She was immediately scheduled for massive doses of chemotherapy, followed by radiation. A bewildering darkness came over us. We instinctively turned to God and waited for a word from Him. The wait seemed endless, yet we knew He would comfort and direct us. Then from our study of God's Word and the encouragement from others came the word in the Scripture below.

> **"Jesus said, 'This sickness will not end in death. No, it is for God's glory so that God's Son may be glorified through it'"** (John 11:4).

This seemed to be God's message to us and to Carrie. God did heal her through His grace. Her restored health brought glory to God and many continue to be encouraged and strengthened by her testimony. Carrie is now living with her own family as a missionary in Germany.

In times of darkness Marilynn and I have chosen to turn to God, and He has been gracious to show us His ways. We sought first to respond in trust and obedience. Each time God has taken us through a crisis, it has called for major adjustments in us and in our walk with Him. But in every case, we've come to a fresh understanding of God and how He wants to work with us. Each time we've been able to take what God has taught us and encourage others.

When times of bewilderment overwhelm you, how you respond will deeply affect your life. Some people withdraw or drop out; others worry and fret, even to the point of becoming sick; still others become angry and bitter. But others turn quietly and persistently to God and wait before Him until He hears their cry and delivers them; they're forever strengthened in their walk with God and they become more faithful servants of His.

When have you experienced a dark time? How were you able to overcome it?

How does God bring light to your difficult times?

JESUS' EXAMPLE

Carefully read Jesus' prayer in Gethsemane and observe the way He dealt with the most difficult hours. Read Matthew 26:36-46 and Hebrews 5:7-10.

How does the way you handle crises compare with the way Jesus dealt with them?

Do you have friends, as Jesus did, to watch with you while you carry your heavy load? If so, how can you encourage them today? If not, what can you do to find such friends?

What do you need to turn over to God right now? Write a prayer to God, giving all your concerns and difficulties to Him right now.

What did God say to you during your study today?

What will you do as a result?

CREATED FOR INTERDEPENDENCE: LIVING WITH GOD'S PEOPLE

"By this all men will know that you are my disciples, if you love one another" (John 13:35).

WHILE RICHARD WAS A UNIVERSITY STUDENT, our church had a Secret Valentine Week. Everyone drew a name and then sent anonymous notes of encouragement throughout the week. The person who drew Richard's name must have left town, because he never received a thing. Richard drew the name of Mrs. Abriel. As a young, single, university student, there were several female names Richard hoped to draw, but the name of an elderly widow living in a rest home wasn't on his list. Although Richard had often seen Mrs. Abriel at church, he'd never talked with her. Swallowing his disappointment, Richard visited her at the senior's residence and, to his surprise, quite enjoyed her company.

During their visit Richard discovered Mrs. Abriel didn't have a regular ride to church; he volunteered to pick her up each Sunday. She had experienced much hardship in her life but had developed a kind, gentle spirit. She would periodically send him encouraging notes and gifts. One weekend Richard went out of town and forgot to tell Mrs. Abriel. When he later apologized for his thoughtlessness, she graciously smiled and told him she had spent a pleasant Sunday morning visiting with people in the rest-home lobby while waiting to be picked up. One day Richard received word that Mrs. Abriel had suffered a stroke and was in intensive care in the hospital. He had never been to the ICU before and was intimidated by the somber atmosphere. When Mrs. Abriel saw him, she gave him a big smile and apologized for being an inconvenience! She thanked him profusely for the time he had taken to visit her. Only a few hours later Mrs. Abriel passed into eternity.

Richard had no idea what a joy it would be to befriend a senior citizen in his church. Her sweet spirit in the midst of her loneliness and pain left an indelible impression upon him and gave him a new appreciation for senior adults. Richard came to understand that belonging to a church family affords opportunities to develop friendships with saints of every age who will greatly enrich your life.

God's invitation to you, not only as a young adult but for the rest of your life, is to join with God's people as He works to redeem a lost world. It's in the midst of the people of God that He refines and develops your character and sends you on mission to the world.

TOGETHER IN INTERDEPENDENCE

> "You are a chosen people, a royal priesthood, a holy nation, a people belonging to God, that you may declare the praises of him who called you out of darkness into his wonderful light. Once you were not a people, but now you are the people of God; once you had not received mercy, but now you have received mercy" (1 Peter 2:9-10).

Derrick had applied to medical school twice; both applications were denied. Bewildered, he came to me (Henry) for counsel. We agreed we would pray and search the Scriptures for direction. Had God closed the door? Was there something lacking in his walk with God? Should he re-apply? Only God could answer these questions. Derrick returned later and assured me that: (1) God had not closed the door, he was certain God wanted him in medicine; and (2) God had given him peace. I sensed something further. I noticed he had not asked his church to pray with him, so we all could experience God's grace through him. He agreed and asked the church to pray. As he once again took the qualifying exams, we all prayed earnestly. This time he passed and entered medical school. Our whole church came to experience new dimensions of confidence in the love and faithfulness of God. Derrick had thought school was something you do on your own. He learned through this experience that as a Christian he was interdependent. He needed others and others needed him. God has made us social beings. We function best when we work with others.

1. SIN'S DESTRUCTION.
Studies consistently reveal that one of society's chief maladies today is loneliness. Sin isolates!

Read Genesis 3:6-24 and Genesis 4:8.

From these verses list eight consequences of man's sin.

Look at your list. How many relationships were affected by sin?

Explain why every sin has the potential for harm.

There's nothing as devastating to the human experience as sin. The first sin, as recorded in Scripture, introduced isolation and separation. Husband and wife now: (1) felt awkward about their intimacy; (2) hid from God, suddenly ashamed to be in His presence; and (3) began to blame each other rather than accept responsibility for their failure. The garden of Eden, once a place of intimacy with God, was closed to humankind. There would subsequently be pain in childbirth. Children would bring heartache to their parents. Animosity developed between brothers, which led to history's first murder. Sin separates people from those who could enrich their lives. Every sin carries this devastating potential. Sin attacks your relationships—with God, with your family, with your friends, with your neighbors. Sin leads you to be independent rather than interdependent. Sin puts all of creation out of joint.

We've counseled college students who lived in the midst of some of the largest campuses and cities in North America, and yet were terribly lonely. Many have wept because of their isolation despite belonging to large families or being surrounded by hundreds of other students. Many notorious murderers and violent criminals have been described as loners. They kept to themselves without counsel or accountability and developed attitudes that were highly destructive to themselves and society. God created mankind with an innate need for togetherness. Our identity and meaning in life are found in the context of our relationships with others. God's invitation is to vital interdependence in the corporate life of His people. This is experienced in many forms but preeminently in a local church body.

Do you have a sense of interdependence with others or do you feel isolated?

Has sin alienated you from someone? If so, how?

Do you find it easy or difficult to be transparent with others? Why?

Sin affirms self and independence, leading to isolation and heartache. But God affirms interdependence, giving and receiving love and forgiveness. These lead to our fulfill-ment, interrelatedness, and mutual significance. Among the people of God you don't lose your identity, as secular critics will try to tell you, but rather it's in the group that your true identity is realized.

2. GOD'S REMEDY

No one is more aware of the pain that sin brings to your relationships than God. That's why He set in motion His plan of redemption.

As you read the following Scripture again, notice God's pattern for a new society, one based on peoples' relationship to Him.

> "You are a chosen people, a royal priesthood, a holy nation, a people belonging to God, that you may declare the praises of him who called you out of darkness into his wonderful light. Once you were not a people, but now you are the people of God; once you had not received mercy, but now you have received mercy" (1 Peter 2:9-10).

What terms does this Scripture use to describe the people of God?

In what ways are they different than before?

In Peter's letter to the churches, he focused on the corporate interdependence of the people of God. Each Christian had an identity as part of God's people. The term *priesthood of believers* is always corporate. As a Christian, you are one priest, belonging to a priesthood. In the Bible, priests were always accountable to one another and functioned together to assist God's people as a whole to be on mission with God. Some have distorted this doctrine to say each person is a priest unto himself and therefore doesn't need others to worship and serve God. Biblically, however, this term always refers to a group of priests.

A PART OF SOMETHING BIGGER
It's a freeing experience to be interdependent with other believers! It's amazing to see this at work in the church. We've seen lonely individuals come alive as they experienced Christian family for the first time. We don't know how many crises our church prayed our young adults through.

In particular, our college students had prayer meetings on campus on Monday, Wednesday, and Friday mornings. They would share what they were facing that day and then pray for each other. When an exam was passed, or an application to a program accepted, the group rejoiced! When a music student had a recital, church members went to show their support. When students participated in sporting events, their church cheered them on. When a student returned from a difficult time spent with their family, they would be comforted by calls and visits from church members. When they went on summer missions, their church family called them and wrote letters, giving a royal welcome when they returned. Whether it was a time of celebration or a time of sorrow, the first place our students wanted to come was to their church! That's because they realized God had made them a vital part of His body. They needed support from their church family, and they knew others needed their encouragement.

This is God's plan: His people, dependent on Him and interdependent on one another.

As a young adult, what are some ways you can be a vital part of God's people, the church?

What did God say to you during your study today?

What will you do as a result?

TOGETHER IN ONE BODY

> "You are the body of Christ, and each one of you is a part of it"
> (1 Corinthians 12:27).

We vividly remember the births of each of our five children. We were thrilled each time God added to our family. Likewise, our church rejoiced every time God added a new member. We were the family of God and we knew it was a sacred moment whenever God blessed us with a new family member.

Read 1 Corinthians 12:27 again. What phrase is used to describe believers? Who is included in this?

When God brought salvation to humankind, He sent us His Son in human form. During that time, people had the awesome privilege of actually seeing, touching, and hearing God (1 John 1). Once Christ ascended to heaven, people could no longer see God in the flesh. Now God takes on physical form by dwelling within His people, the church. The church has become God's new earthly body. This has significant implications. To see God today, people are to look to the church. They see God's love by watching how Christians love each other. They see God's power by observing Him do the impossible through His church.

Local churches are the visible expression of the body of Christ. It's through these churches that God seeks to carry out His plan to bring salvation to mankind. In the Scripture below, notice what happens, according to Paul, when you join a church.

> "In fact God has arranged the parts in the body, every one of them, just as he wanted them to be" (1 Corinthians 12:18).

According to this verse, how does God build a church?

How personally is God involved in the church?

GOD EQUIPS THE CHURCH

The churches where we pastored took their responsibility to new church members seriously. We would ask each new member to commit to the entire church to allow God to use them to "build up" His church. We would then challenge the other members to encourage and pray for the new member so that together we could function as God's body and accomplish His purpose.

Each church is Christ's body and He has particular assignments for it. Because we are His body on earth, He will carry out His redemptive work through us. Further, He will equip each church to carry out His assignment. For instance, If God wants to reach the disadvantaged people of a downtown area, He may choose to do so through your church. In this case, He will sensitize your church to that particular need and then equip it to minister. God knows what His assignment for each church will be, so He adds members whom He intends to use in these ministries. God places people in churches for a reason. It is so they can do their part as a member of the body and, together, carry out God's assignment for it.

It was always exciting to see who God added to our church. A musician would give her talents to playing the piano during worship services. An actor would organize a drama team to enhance our worship. Future educators would become Sunday School teachers. An artist designed the church brochure and sign. An architect planned the addition to our church building. Young ministers preached in our missions. Other young adults devoted their energies to working with our youth. Some served as ushers or labored on the church grounds. Some sang in the choir; many served on committees. Those gifted with compassion would go to rest homes and minister to the elderly. Some who had come out of a life of alcohol and drug abuse would lead services in the rescue mission downtown. Each young adult who joined was challenged to discover why God brought him or her to our church, and other members would then become involved in the work God did through these new members.

Our church had several young boys who came from broken homes. God burdened a college student named Tom for these boys. Tom was especially concerned about those who had no father in their house. He taught some to play musical instruments and encouraged all of them to live a Christian life that would honor God. He even volunteered at their schools. There were many boys whose world Tom brightened. He became the strong Christian role model these kids desperately needed at a critical time in their lives. There are young men scattered throughout the world today who still write and visit him. Many have married Christian women and have successful careers. Through Tom's concern for these boys, our church developed various ministries to these children and their families. God equipped the church for this ministry through Tom.

When God places you in a local church, you're not merely joining a religious organization; you're part of the living body of Christ. God puts you in a particular church because He knows you can help that church fulfill His assignment. You're vital to the body and the body is important to you.

NO DIVISION

Notice in the Scripture below one aspect of this relationship with God in His body.

> "... so that there should be no division in the body, but that its parts should have equal concern for each other. If one part suffers, every part suffers with it; if one part is honored, every part rejoices with it" (1 Corinthians 12:25-26).

According to this verse, if someone in your church faces a painful situation, how should you respond?

If someone in your church is experiencing joy or success, how should it affect you?

Our church sought to function in a way that reflected the above passage. When Joe graduated from the college of medicine, we had a fellowship celebration. When Dan won an award in fine arts, many attended the art show rejoicing because we were so proud of him. When Debbie's mother died of cancer, we gathered around to give comfort.

Brenda was ostracized by her own family for becoming a Christian, so we wept with her and surrounded her with the love of Christ. One Sunday evening, a young couple stood before the church and wept as they confessed their sexual sin. They received forgiveness as those present offered their love and prayed that they would experience restoration. People discovered that as a part of the body of Christ you don't hurt alone. Likewise, your church family shares your joys and successes. Take careful note: Watching religious programs online or reading Christian books can never replace your church family!

> GOD PUTS YOU IN A PARTICULAR CHURCH BECAUSE
> HE KNOWS YOU CAN HELP THAT CHURCH FULFILL
> HIS ASSIGNMENT. YOU ARE VITAL TO THE BODY
> AND THE BODY IS IMPORTANT TO YOU.

Read Ephesians 4:1-3,11-14 to see how Paul describes the church. Make a list of ways others build you up.

If you left town for a month, what ministries within your church would suffer?

How might God use you to build up ...

Teenagers: Families:

Senior adults: Other young adults:

What did God say to you during your study today?

What will you do as a result?

TOGETHER IN CARING

> "Bear with each other and forgive whatever grievances you may have against one another. Forgive as the Lord forgave you" (Colossians 3:13).

One Sunday evening while I (Richard) was a college student, I was sitting in church waiting for the service to begin. Across the auditorium sat Mrs. Clark, a tiny, frail woman recently widowed. A thought came to me: *Now that Mr. Clark is gone, who will maintain her yard?* I dismissed the thought and resumed reading the order of service in the bulletin. The question came again: *Who will help Mrs. Clark?* I finally rose and made my way over to Mrs. Clark. When I told her about my concern for the upkeep of her yard, I was taken aback by the look of joy and relief that spread across her face. Mrs. Clark was a gracious woman who refused to be a burden to anyone. Yet she felt overwhelmed by trying to maintain her large yard without her husband and had been praying that God would send help. In exchange for my yard work, Mrs. Clark gave me a box of her famous baked goodies, which I (and my three roommates) eagerly looked forward to each week. Mrs. Clark became a blessing to me and my roommates even as she had been blessed.

When my son Mike was 10 years old, he commented, "What do people do who don't have a church? I feel sorry for them." He was insightful to realize so young that the church is indispensable for the Christian. In this lesson we will examine three areas where church members can effectively minister to one another.

1. HELPING ONE ANOTHER
Read Acts 4:33-35.

How did the church respond to people in need? Why do you think they did this?

How willing are you to part with your possessions to help someone in your church?

Has someone in your church met a need in your life? If so, write and mail them a brief note. Then thank God for expressing His love for you through that person.

NO SHORTAGE OF NEEDS

The churches where we pastored were always filled with needy people. Muriel was an elderly lady with multiple sclerosis. She was in a wheelchair and had great difficulty speaking. Our church family came to know Muriel well enough that they could understand what she was saying, and they became actively involved in her life. Our young church members saw her as a special person. They would give her rides to church, and someone would always sit with her during the service. They would take her on outings on the weekends. She was often invited to birthday parties. We believed it was no accident that God added several medical students to our church family who understood her condition and were able to minister to her. This lonely woman's life received an enormous blessing from the young adults at our church, and they grew spiritually as they ministered to her.

We also had several people who were mentally challenged. Some of our church members volunteered to teach a special Bible study and minister to them during the week. Many of our young adults would go out of their way to befriend those who were neglected at home and in society. These special people found love and acceptance at our church that they had not discovered anywhere else.

Young adults can be extremely creative! Peter had little money, but he wanted to help young families at his church. He designed homemade coupons and gave them as gifts to young parents. His coupons could be redeemed for free baby-sitting, raking leaves, or errands for the busy parents. Peter allowed the Spirit of God to guide him in practical ways to minister to others in his church.

God blessed us with mature adults who ministered to our university students. We had a Ukrainian lady in our church who loved to cook for them. Some of the meals she served were legendary! There were families who regularly invited international students into their homes for Christmas and other holidays. Some helped students find summer jobs. Many of our young adults developed friendships with church members that lasted long into adulthood. Together as a church, we sought to meet one another's needs.

2. FORGIVING ONE ANOTHER

Read the Scriptures below.

> "Bear with each other and forgive whatever grievances you may have against one another. Forgive as the Lord forgave you" (Colossians 3:13).

> "Brothers, if someone is caught in a sin, you who are spiritual should restore him gently. But watch yourself, or you also may be tempted. Carry each other's burdens, and in this way you will fulfill the law of Christ" (Galatians 6:1-2).

What conflicts did the first church face?

How does Scripture say you should respond to someone with whom you have a grievance?

How were church members to respond to someone caught in sin?

Do you have a church family that supports you? How do they do that? Will you trust them to help you?

What are you doing to help a fellow church member who has a burden?

The early churches were not immune to conflicts. Yet Paul admonished them to bear with one another, making allowances for each other's imperfections. He further instructed them to forgive in the same way Christ forgave them. Anyone who realizes the awesome cost involved for God to forgive their sin will consider it a small thing to forgive the often trivial offenses of others.

3. PRAYING FOR ONE ANOTHER

Read James 5:14-16. Why is it important to pray for one another?

How seriously do you take the prayer concerns of fellow Christians? How do you respond to those prayer concerns?

Do you take advantage of opportunities in your faith community to pray for those who need healing or forgiveness? Explain.

There's no better place on earth to share your concerns than with your church family. They can take your needs into the throne room of God and ask for His divine intervention for your life. Miracles have occurred as the result of church prayer meetings! When couples announced their engagement in our church, they often would come before the congregation and we would commit to pray for them as they approached their marriage. Ivah, an elderly widow, loved to pray. When a student in our church had a difficult assignment or they were going to share the gospel with a friend, they would always alert Ivah so they would have the assurance of her intercession.

List the ways church members can minister to one another.

What did God say to you during your study today?

What will you do as a result?

TOGETHER IN FELLOWSHIP

> "They devoted themselves to the apostles' teaching and to the fellowship, to the breaking of bread and to prayer. Everyone was filled with awe, and many wonders and miraculous signs were done by the apostles. All the believers were together and had everything in common. Every day they continued to meet together in the temple courts. They broke bread in their homes and ate together with glad and sincere hearts, praising God and enjoying the favor of all the people. And the Lord added to their number daily those who were being saved" (Acts 2:42-44,46-47).

In AD 320, the Roman Emperor Licinius commanded Christians to renounce their faith or be executed. Forty soldiers stationed at Sebaste, Armenia, in the Twelfth Legion refused the command. They were stripped naked and forced out onto a frozen lake. On the shore Roman soldiers built fires and prepared warm baths for anyone willing to recant and forsake Christianity. In their final hours of life, those 40 believers sang hymns and prayed together. Finally, one of them was so overcome with fear and cold that he fled to the shore. However, a soldier on the shoreline had been so impressed by the dedication and fellowship of the faithful Christians that he ran out to join them, replacing the defector. Their devotion to Christ and their love for one another had been so compelling that an observer was inspired to give his life to Christ. The fellowship between Christians and their God can have a powerful, life-changing influence on others. Young adults who have participated in such fellowship have had their lives changed forever.[1]

Read in Acts 2:42-44,46-47 the description of the first church God established.

What words come to mind as you read how the first church functioned?

In Acts 2:42 what were the four things to which the church members devoted themselves?

What evidence suggests the people cared for one another?

How did all of this affect those who were watching them?

Scripture gives a glimpse of how the early churches functioned. They did everything together. They studied God's Word together at the feet of the apostles. They fellowshipped together at the temple or in each other's homes. They broke bread together. They also prayed together. The result was that unbelievers observing them were attracted to what they saw and people were regularly being converted and joining them.

KOINONIA

The fact that early Christians met together is not unusual; pagan religions did the same thing. The difference was in the *koinonia* that the first church experienced. The Greek word *koinonia* is one of the most exciting words in the New Testament. It means the total interrelatedness in love between God and those He loves. No English word can fully express it. Notice how the Amplified Bible translates it in 1 John 1:

> **"What we have seen and [ourselves] heard we are also telling you, so that you too may realize *and* enjoy fellowship as partners *and* partakers with us. And [this] fellowship that we have (which is a distinguishing mark of Christians) is with the Father and with His Son Jesus Christ, the Messiah" (v. 3, AMP).**

What is the distinguishing mark of Christians?

With whom do Christians have fellowship?

John was one of Jesus' closest friends. In the above verse John invited every person to enjoy an intimate fellowship with God. Notice the close connection between our relationship with God and our relationship with other Christians in the Scripture below.

> "... that all of them may be one, Father, just as you are in me and I am in you. May they also be in us so that the world may believe that you have sent me. I have given them the glory that you gave me, that they may be one as we are one: I in them and you in me. May they be brought to complete unity to let the world know that you sent me and have loved them even as you have loved me" (John 17:21-23).

Write the essence of Jesus' prayer in one sentence.

What's the model for how unified Christians are to be?

What will be the result of perfect unity among believers?

We cannot fathom the intimacy between God the Father and God the Son. The Father loved His Son with a holy, perfect love. Christ loved His Heavenly Father perfectly and was absolutely submissive to His will. Their hearts, minds, and wills were in complete harmony.

Because of this, Jesus prayed in John 17 that each of His followers would be devoted to God the Father and to the Son in the same way that the Father and Son loved each other.

As Christians experience the incredible, sacrificial love of God, they naturally want to respond in love. Christians have the same Heavenly Father and are spiritually brothers and sisters. It is this mutual relationship to our Lord that leads to a divine fellowship, or *koinonia,* a fellowship we experience with God and with each other.

There are several areas where *koinonia* is expressed in the church. These include prayer, worship, and gathering together.

1. FELLOWSHIP IN PRAYER

A fascinating event occurred in the first church in Acts 12. Notice the Scripture below.

> **"Peter was kept in prison, but the church was earnestly praying to God for him. When this [miraculous release from prison] had dawned on him, he went to the house of Mary the mother of John, also called Mark, where many people had gathered and were praying. But Peter kept on knocking, and when they opened the door and saw him, they were astonished" (vv. 5,12,16).**

What was Peter's situation?

How did the church respond to Peter's dilemma?

Peter faced one of the darkest times of his life. Imprisoned by King Herod, he was scheduled to be executed. The church immediately assembled at the home of John Mark's mother and prayed through the night. As they were praying, Peter knocked on the door! The people were amazed and grew even stronger in their faith in God and their commitment to one another.

Prayer meetings were special times of intimacy in our church. Young adults made up a large percentage of the group that gathered weekly to encourage one another. The gathering would often last two hours or longer. We sat in a circle and searched God's Word for fresh insights for our life together as the body of Christ. We shared what we saw God doing around us. We were alert to the Holy Spirit as He sensitized our hearts to one another.

> AS CHRISTIANS EXPERIENCE THE INCREDIBLE,
> SACRIFICIAL LOVE OF GOD,
> THEY NATURALLY WANT TO RESPOND IN LOVE.

We would divide into small groups to pray for one another. Many of our church members shared their burdens for non-Christian parents, family, and friends. Some confessed and repented of their sins and experienced the joy that comes from forgiveness. Others prayed about jobs, school, illness, finances, or relationships. When someone told what they were experiencing, others often felt impressed by the Spirit to pray with them and to encourage them during the week. As the formal prayer time closed, many groups continued to pray. It was not uncommon for young adults to come to a saving faith in Christ during the prayer meeting. So intimate and exciting was this time that many would bring their friends to the prayer meeting before ever inviting them to a worship service!

This experience is God's invitation for His people. Our Lord was present with us, guiding and instructing us in our life together. His life was expressed and authentically experienced in us, among us, and through us to a watching, hurting, searching world. The closer and more transparent our love-relationship with God, the more intimate and real is our love-relationship with His people. This is why our prayer meetings were so meaningful. They grew from the intimacy of our fellowship with God!

How would you describe the fellowship you have with God? Circle all that apply.

Joyful	Awkward	Uninspiring
Rewarding	Exciting	Uneventful
Inspiring	Powerful	Nonexistent

How would you describe your fellowship with other believers?

Warm	Joyful	Tense
Awkward	Encouraging	Exciting
Healing	Growing	Stagnant

2. FELLOWSHIP IN WORSHIP

In addition to prayer, *koinonia* is also expressed through corporate worship.

Carefully read about the unusual worship service conducted by Paul and Silas in Acts 16:22-26.

What hardships described in this passage did Paul and Silas experience?

What did Paul and Silas do after being jailed? What was the result?

Paul and Silas had been falsely accused, publicly humiliated, brutally beaten, and illegally imprisoned under maximum security. In spite of all this, they worshiped and praised God! This certainly got the attention of those around them. Then God released His awesome power. Many stories are told of Christians who, in difficult circumstances, gathered together and worshiped God. As they did, their love for God and one another grew to divine proportions and the power of God was released in their midst.

Our church often experienced *koinonia* during worship times as God granted us a powerful sense of His presence. Together we learned the meaning of Proverbs 9:10, which says, "The fear of the LORD is the beginning of wisdom, and knowledge of the Holy One is understanding." Week after week in the presence of Holy God, young adults would examine the will of God in their lives. Some would respond to God's call to enter medicine, engineering, or Christian ministry and missions. Couples would dedicate their relationship to God before the entire church. The Holy Spirit would use God's Word to teach people about sin, righteousness, and judgment (John 16:8-9).

THE HOLY SPIRIT GUIDES PEOPLE TO A COMMON GOAL
AND PURPOSE TO ACCOMPLISH HIS DESIRES.

A HEART YIELDED IN WORSHIP

One Sunday as we ended our morning service, a young man came to the front of the church and said with great emotion, "God has been calling me into full-time Christian ministry but I've been running from His call. Today I've stopped running. I want my church to know I'm surrendering my life to God's will, wherever He leads!" His testimony impacted several other young people in the church.

Because of the intimate fellowship of the church body, the anguish of this student over his own disobedience convicted others that they, too, had been slow to respond to God's call. These also stood and shared the commitments they were making to the Lord that morning. The whole church family was encouraged, for we had been praying for "the Lord of the harvest" to "send out workers" (Matthew 9:38) and we saw God answer our prayers that day. We stood in awe as we realized that Almighty God had intervened in our little church that morning.

3. FELLOWSHIP IN GATHERING TOGETHER

> **"I tell you that if two of you on earth agree about anything you ask for,
> it will be done for you by my Father in heaven. For where two or three
> come together in my name, there am I with them" (Matthew 18:18-19).**

What are the criteria for God answering your prayers?

Where does God promise to be present?

In this often-quoted passage, Jesus extended two promises. First, He said that when two or more Christians seek the mind of God together in prayer, He will grant their requests. The reason isn't that God automatically grants the requests of groups of Christians. It's because the Holy Spirit guides people to a common goal and purpose to accomplish His desires. Second, although God is always with His children, Jesus said there's a dimension to His presence which can be felt only when Christians gather together and are of one heart and purpose. Koinonia can be experienced in any situation or circumstance where two or more Christians gather and are united by the Holy Spirit.

We've seen young adults discover this *koinonia* in numerous ways. Some gathered in a friend's hospital room shortly before she was to have surgery. As they prayed for and encouraged her, a joy was evident that caused even non-Christian nurses to sense God's presence in the room. Greg was moments away from taking a three-hour oral exam when he suddenly was surrounded by friends from his church. They had an impromptu prayer meeting in the conference room that soon would be the scene of the most important exam of his life. We knew three young adults who met in a restaurant to minister to each other. In the midst of their conversation, a non-Christian from the next booth approached them and awkwardly asked if she might join them. She had been listening and wanted to participate in the loving counsel she had overheard. The prayer room in our church became a frequent gathering place for young adults as two or three would pray for each other in times of difficulty. Groups would gather after church services or prayer meetings and enjoy such a wonderful time of fellowship that they were reluctant to go home.

There's nothing in this life like the *koinonia* that comes from fellowship with God and fellow believers. It's a taste of heaven on earth!

Do you regularly experience the *koinonia* discussed in this lesson? If you answered yes, describe what the *koinonia* experience is like.

How can you encourage other young adults to participate in this fellowship?

In what ways can you isolate yourself from meaningful fellowship with other believers? What influence can this have on *koinonia*?

Do you trust the people of God? How can you make your life more open to fellow Christians?

What did God say to you during your study today?

What will you do as a result?

TOGETHER IN MISSIONS

> "We are therefore Christ's ambassadors, as though God were making his appeal through us. We implore you on Christ's behalf: Be reconciled to God" (2 Corinthians 5:20).

In 1727 a church of 300 people gathered in Herrnhut, Saxony. There had been little spiritual power evident in this church's early days. However, the young pastor, Nicolas Zinzendorf, called on the people to pray. On August 27 24 men and 24 women committed to pray around the clock. This unbroken prayer time lasted for more than 100 years! Six months after their prayers began, the Holy Spirit was working so powerfully among them that the pastor asked if any were willing to release their lives to God in missions to the West Indies, Greenland, Turkey, and Lapland. The next day 26 people stepped forward, committing their lives to spreading the gospel around the world. By 1792 that church of 300 had sent 300 missionaries around the world. They ministered to groups of people never previously reached by the gospel. One Moravian missionary (as they were called) had a life-changing influence on John and Charles Wesley, which led to their conversions. They in turn were influential in the Great Awakening throughout England and North America during the 1700s. Many years later when the modern mission movement began, missionaries would arrive in remote parts of the world and discover that a missionary from that small church had already been there. One small church chose to go on mission with God and He used them to impact the world.[2]

God's invitation to you is to join His work to redeem people and to impact a world through your church. Notice what Paul said about the churches of his day in the Scriptures below.

> "We are therefore Christ's ambassadors, as though God were making his appeal through us. We implore you on Christ's behalf: Be reconciled to God" (2 Corinthians 5:20).

> "As God's fellow workers we urge you not to receive God's grace in vain. For he says, 'In the time of my favor I heard you, and in the day of salvation I helped you.' I tell you, now is the time of God's favor, now is the day of salvation" (2 Corinthians 6:1-2).

According to the previous Scripture, what did Paul say every Christian was supposed to do?

According to 2 Corinthians 6:1, with whom are you working?

In Scripture we see that the heart and purpose of God is for the people of God to be on mission with Him. The Great Commission and the promise of the Holy Spirit was given to the people of God, together in the churches.

UNDER CHRIST'S DIRECTION

Read Ephesians 1:17-23. List the things Paul prayed.

What did God do according to verse 22? Who did He do this for?

How is the church described in verse 23?

Paul prayed not only that they would come to know God better, but that they would realize the glorious inheritance that was theirs as members of the saints. He prayed they would realize the "incomparably great power" that had been placed in Christ. Christ now rules the universe. God has placed everything under Christ's control and has done this for the church, which is His body. The risen, triumphant Lord has been given to the church as its Head. Christ directs the church to fulfill God's plans to redeem humankind. Christ Himself directs His church. What more exciting group could you be a part of than this?

OUR MISSION

While we ministered in Canada, we faced a big challenge. Canada was largely apathetic to the gospel and only a small minority of its people were Christians. Our church was small and had limited resources. Yet Christ, the Head of our church, led us to seek to evangelize our nation for Him. He directed us to cities, towns, and villages where there was no gospel witness and provided the resources to begin churches, build buildings, and send preachers and Bible teachers to those who needed to hear the good news of Christ.

Our young adults were part of a church that was on mission with God to redeem an entire nation and the world. When we began a new mission church, God would call out some to be involved in that work. These young adults would agree to go each Sunday to teach Sunday School at the mission. Others would go to play the piano or make outreach visits. Some would work with youth while others would occasionally preach.

CHRIST NOW RULES THE UNIVERSE.
GOD HAS PLACED EVERYTHING UNDER CHRIST'S CONTROL
AND HAS DONE THIS FOR THE CHURCH,
WHICH IS HIS BODY.

At times the efforts of young adults could be quite humorous. One nervous young man drove two hours to preach at a mission. At the front of the little auditorium was a makeshift pulpit, consisting of a table topped with a portable lectern to hold the preacher's notes. In front of the lectern was a beautiful flower arrangement. As our preacher-in-training nervously gripped the lectern, he was oblivious to the fact that it was nudging the flower arrangement closer and closer to the edge of the table. At a climactic moment in his sermon, he sent the flowers crashing to the floor! Aghast, he raced around the table and frantically tried to reassemble the flower arrangement as the congregation struggled to suppress their laughter! This student went on to become a pastor and continues to serve the Lord faithfully.

Another young adult volunteered to live in a native Indian community to minister to the people there. In his attempt to control the acres of grassland surrounding the humble parsonage, he set the field on fire. Whipped by wind and unhindered by water (since the young pastor had neglected to secure hoses), the fire threatened to engulf the entire community! Today he is in full-time Christian ministry.

One of our mission churches invited a student to preach one Sunday. As he drove over unmarked country roads, he took a wrong turn. Approaching the town just in time for the service, he noticed a sign welcoming him to Lanigan. He was supposed to be preaching in Leroy! Panicking, he turned around and raced across the gravel roads, screeching into Leroy at 11:30. A fellow student, there to direct the music, was leading the congregation in prayer, planning to pray as long as he had to until the preacher arrived. As the flustered preacher burst into the sanctuary, he was met with a not-too-spiritual glare by the music director. Nevertheless, God blessed their efforts; they both are in full-time ministry today.

We could tell you story after story of the ministry efforts of our young adults and how God used them in spite of themselves. Their ability never mattered as much as their availability. They recognized that Christ was their Head and whatever He assigned them to do, He also would enable them to accomplish it. He could overcome their limitations! Together the young adults in our church watched God build His kingdom across the land. God's invitation to you is for you to link your life with His church and then to be on mission with Him.

THE WISDOM OF GOD
Read Ephesians 3:8-12,21.

What was Paul assigned to do (vv. 8-9)?

What vehicle does God use to display His wisdom (v. 10)?

To whom did God display His wisdom?

Where will God's glory be "for ever and ever" (v. 21)?

In light of these verses, how important is it that you be involved in a church as God planned?

Paul had received clear instructions from the Head of the church regarding his assignment, to proclaim to the Gentiles the "unending (boundless, fathomless, incalculable, and exhaustless) riches of Christ" (v. 8, AMP). He also was to teach them that God's plan from the beginning was to reveal His infinite wisdom to all the angelic powers and principalities through the church. Does that mean the church is perfect? No! But it does mean that God has designed the church with a special purpose that will happen nowhere else. It's through the church's obedience and worship that God receives glory and demonstrates His wisdom to all the universe.

I (Henry) was the pastor of a church in one of the highest crime areas of San Francisco. Our community was filled with drugs, violence, crime, and divorce. As a young pastor, I couldn't begin to provide answers for the plethora of need that surrounded our congregation. One night there was a domestic quarrel in our neighborhood in which the husband barricaded himself in his home with a shotgun. The police turned to our church for help, and God used us to help bring about a peaceful resolution. One evening the worship service was interrupted by 23 bikers from a gang called the Untouchables, who brazenly sauntered into the back of the church and sat down. All 23 leaned back in their chairs, defying the church to affect them. But God had other plans! Within a year, all but one had given their hearts to Christ as their Savior. We saw young people addicted to drugs and alcohol released from their bondage. We witnessed marriages that were virtually over restored through the ministry of Christ in our church. People suffering debilitating depression found joy for the first time in the fellowship of our church family. Those who had never before experienced unconditional love found themselves surrounded by God's love through His people.

How can God use your church to impact your community?

What must you adjust in your life in order to be a part of God's redemptive plan for your church?

What did God say to you during your study today?

What will you do as a result?

7

KINGDOM LIVING: GETTING THE BIGGER PICTURE

"Seek first his kingdom and his righteousness, and all these things will be given to you as well" (Matthew 6:33).

KINGDOM CITIZENS

ALL OVER PANAMA CITY BEACH, FLORIDA, cold beer was consumed by the truckload, and sunbathers partied till they dropped during spring break. At the same time, God had invited a group of Christian college students to reach out to those who needed to know God's love. They call this event BeachReach, an annual outreach effort that has affected those hurting and searching for meaning for years.

This particular year almost eight hundred college students from 50 different campuses gave up their spring break and, many at their own expense, traveled to Florida to share Christ. They offered a free pancake breakfast every morning, van rides for those too drunk to drive, and a crisis-intervention hotline for students who had reached the bottom. Many students gave their lives to Christ. Four runaways, as young as 13 years old, accepted Christ as Lord and Savior and returned home. One student who became a Christian during the last van ride of the week said he had heard the gospel from six different Christians and concluded, "They seemed to be the only truly happy people here!" One group was pursuing hedonistic pleasures. The emptier they felt, the harder they partied. The other belonged to Christ; their pleasure came from honoring God and serving Him.

THE KINGDOM'S QUALITIES

> "The kingdom of heaven is like treasure hidden in a field. When a man found it, he hid it again, and then in his joy went and sold all he had and bought that field" (Matthew 13:44).

What is your greatest priority? Rank these from 1 to 7, with 1 being the most important.

___ Going to heaven when you die

___ Seeking the kingdom of God

___ Being happy

___ Getting married

___ Pursuing a successful career

___ Having children

___ Fulfilling your dreams

Did you mark seeking the kingdom of God as number one? If so, did you put it first because you knew it was the right answer?

Most of us are familiar with this session's memory verse, but do we really know what it means? If you're to seek first the kingdom of God, it's important that you understand what this kingdom is like. The kingdom of God is His rule over all creation. He controls the universe, and every person ultimately will give an account of their lives to Him. Every believer in every part of the world is a citizen of the kingdom. Every church where the gospel is proclaimed belongs to the kingdom.

A KINGDOM INVITATION

In Matthew 13 Jesus gave several descriptions of what the kingdom of God means. As He did, He warned that not everyone would understand the "secrets of the kingdom" (v. 11) but only those who were its citizens. Jesus also recognized that people would respond differently to the invitation from the king. Before studying the qualities of the kingdom, notice the various ways people respond to it, as described in Matthew 13.

"A farmer went out to sow his seed. As he was scattering the seed, some fell along the path, and the birds came and ate it up. Some fell on rocky places, where it did not have much soil. It sprang up quickly, because the soil was shallow. But when the sun came up, the plants were scorched, and they withered because they had no root. Other seed fell among thorns, which grew up and choked the plants. Still other seed fell on good soil, where it produced a crop—a hundred, sixty or thirty times what was sown" (vv. 3-8).

In the Scripture, circle the four results of sowing seed.

Jesus said this parable illustrates four ways people respond to God's invitation. What four responses do you see? Underline them.

When Jesus began His public ministry, He preached, "Repent, for the kingdom of heaven is near" (Matthew 4:17). Everywhere Jesus went He gave the same invitation: for people to become citizens of the kingdom of God. Some rejected His invitation and even went as far as crucifying Him. Others expressed interest, but were not willing to pay the price. Others began to respond to the invitation of the gospel, but the cares and concerns of the world choked out their initial interest. However, there were those who willingly accepted the responsibilities of kingdom citizenship and God produced a great spiritual crop through their lives. The invitation to the kingdom of God is given to everyone. The difference is in our response.

KINGDOM QUALITIES

Edward Kimball was a Sunday School teacher in a Congregationalist church in Boston where he taught a class for teenage boys. Convicted by the Holy Spirit that he did not know the spiritual condition of each of his students, he began to visit them individually to find out if they were Christians. Kimball visited the shoe store where one of his class members, an 18-year-old named Dwight, worked. In the room where he stocked shelves, Dwight Lyman Moody (1837–99), gave his life to Christ. He went on to become an international evangelist, preaching to more than 130,000 people in one day! He founded three schools and two publishing houses. It's estimated that in his lifetime, Moody traveled more than one million miles and preached the gospel to 100 million people.

One of those converted under Moody's ministry was John Wilbur Chapman (1859–1918); he too became a full-time evangelist. In addition, he wrote or edited 30 books and numerous pamphlets on the Christian life. William Ashley Sunday (1862–1935), a professional baseball player, was converted as a result of Chapman's ministry and also became a full-time evangelist. It's estimated that 300,000 people gave their lives to Christ during his evangelistic meetings. One of the converts in Sunday's ministry was Mordecai Fowler Ham (1877–1961). Ham devoted his life to preaching the gospel and saw hundreds of thousands of conversions. During a revival meeting in 1934 in Charlotte, North Carolina, William Frank Graham (1918–2018) was converted. Billy Graham was a shy 16-year-old—an unlikely candidate for international ministry. However, as a teenager, he committed his life entirely to God's service and prayed that God might use him in His kingdom work. During Billy Graham's ministry, hundreds of millions of people have heard the gospel message and millions have responded in faith. On April 14, 1996, an estimated 2.5 billion people in 160 countries heard him present the gospel, which was translated into 42 languages.

Did Edward Kimball know what would come of his obedience in 1855? Of course not. Did God? Certainly! Kimball was obedient to what God invited him to do and God used his obedience to bring millions into His kingdom. Every act of obedience carries with it the potential to mightily impact the kingdom of God. God invites you to obey His instructions for your life and to experience Him working in you to bring a world to Christ.

Notice what Jesus said the qualities of the kingdom would be like in Matthew 13.

1. THE KINGDOM STARTS OUT SMALL
Read Matthew 13:31-32.

According to this parable, how does kingdom work begin?

How large does the work of the kingdom become?

Does size indicate success in God's kingdom? Why or why not?

You may be discouraged if your Christian student group is small or your church is not as large as others. Don't be. God chooses to work through the small and weak to demonstrate His power to a watching world. Small beginnings do not necessarily mean a small finish. Most of God's greatest works have begun small, like the mustard seed.

2. THE KINGDOM HAS A STEADY INFLUENCE
Read the verse below.

> "The kingdom of heaven is like yeast that a woman took and mixed into a large amount of flour until it worked all through the dough" (Matthew 13:33).

How does yeast operate in a batch of dough?

How would this apply to the work of God in society?

Yeast isn't significant by itself. It's not flashy. It doesn't work in a loud, flamboyant way. But it gets the job done. One moment there's a small lump of dough, sitting inconspicuously in a bowl. Check a couple of hours later and the dough is bulging over the top and down the sides. God's kingdom works that way; He needs no marketing experts to help His kingdom have an impact! God works behind the scenes, saving people one at a time.

This happened in China. When the communists expelled all the Christian missionaries, many feared Christianity would be extinguished in that country. Four decades later the Western world discovered, to its surprise, more than 100 million Christians! What happened? The kingdom of God had steadily grown, quietly spreading throughout the country. Your witness in your corner of the world will be similar. You may not always see instant or dramatic results to all you do, but God will take your efforts and work in the lives of people of whom you might not even be aware.

3. IT HAS GREAT VALUE
Read the verses below.

> "The kingdom of heaven is like treasure hidden in a field. When a man found it, he hid it again, and then in his joy went and sold all he had and bought that field" (Matthew 13:44).

> "Again, the kingdom of heaven is like a merchant looking for fine pearls. When he found one of great value, he went away and sold everything he had and bought it" (Matthew 13:45-46).

In what two ways did Jesus describe the kingdom of God?

How important was the kingdom of God to the people in the stories? How do you know?

Jesus was teaching that becoming a citizen of the kingdom is the most important thing you will ever do. If becoming a Christian meant that you had to give up everything else, it would be worth it. We had young adults join our church who paid a great price for their commitment to Christ. Their family members would ostracize them; parents would expel them from their homes; friends would forsake them; relatives would boycott their weddings; and much more. We counseled many who faced the painful truth that sometimes you must decide if the kingdom of God is more important than anything else. These young adults were convinced it was, and God gave them the courage to stick to their decision.

4. IT HAS ETERNAL DIMENSIONS
Read Matthew 13:47-50.

Whom do the two kinds of fish represent in Jesus' parable?

What are their two destinations?

When a fisherman draws in his nets, there are both good and bad fish (see also Matthew 13:24-30). For a time the fisherman allows the bad fish to remain with the good. But before he brings the fish home he discards the worthless fish. Jesus was saying that the final judgment isn't immediate, but it's definite. Kingdom citizens may even face persecution by non-citizens for a time. The wicked may prosper while the righteous suffer. Ultimately, however, God is absolutely just. You may feel surrounded by the forces of evil. Yet, Jesus assures His citizens that He has won the victory and that ultimately those who reject His invitation to the kingdom will be punished.

> JESUS TAUGHT THAT BECOMING A CITIZEN OF THE KINGDOM
> IS THE MOST IMPORTANT THING YOU WILL EVER DO.
> IF BECOMING A CHRISTIAN MEANT YOU HAD TO
> GIVE UP EVERYTHING ELSE, IT WOULD BE WORTH IT.

Do you find comfort in the fact that God will be absolutely just in His judgment of you? Explain.

How are you living your life as a kingdom citizen?

The rules of God's kingdom are usually contradictory to the commonly held beliefs of modern society. In the exercise below, place a *K* beside the principles of God's kingdom and a *W* beside the things commonly taught by the world.

____ Size is the best indicator of success.

____ Marketing is everything!

____ What is important is obedience.

____ Do whatever makes you happy!

____ The key to success is a heart that is right toward God.

____ Live for eternity, not time.

PRINCE OR PAUPER?

Mark Twain told the delightful tale of two boys who, by freak circumstances, had their roles reversed. One was a pauper, living in dire poverty, abused and suffering hardship. The other was a prince who lived in comfort and luxury. When they switched places, the prince was forced to live the life of a beggar, while the pauper was pampered and coddled. The frustrated prince was forced to live far below the means he knew were his.

Unfortunately, many Christians live like paupers when they are sons and daughters of the King. They live on meager spiritual resources and suffer constant defeat. In reality they are children of the King and therefore have access to all His resources. God has given His children everything they need. It would be a tragedy to live with anything less. (See Romans 8:14-17; 2 Corinthians 1:20; Ephesians 1:3; 2:4-7.)

What evidence in your life demonstrates that you are a child of the King?

What did God say to you during your study today?

What will you do as a result?

THE KINGDOM'S KEYS

> "I will give you the keys of the kingdom of heaven; whatever you bind
> on earth will be bound in heaven, and whatever you loose on earth will
> be loosed in heaven" (Matthew 16:19).

I (Henry) had one of the most embarrassing and frustrating experiences of my life when I flew to Richmond, Virginia, to speak at a conference recently. There was a terrible snowstorm and I was eager to arrive at the conference center. I rented a new car with every modern, convenient device available. I felt certain that if any vehicle could maneuver through the storm that day, it would be this one. Nevertheless, the car became stuck in a snowdrift. Having lived many years on the Canadian prairies, I felt I was somewhat of an expert in freeing snowbound cars! From experience I knew my strategy would differ depending on whether the car was front- or rear-wheel drive. I wasn't sure which type of car this was, so not knowing any other way to tell which tires were spinning in the snow, I left the car in drive, and got out to take a look. The wind was howling around me and the snow was blinding. Peering at the wheels I determined which tires were spinning uselessly in an icy rut. Shivering in the cold, I hurried to get back in the car. Just then, a strong wind seized the car door and slammed it shut. As soon as the door closed, the doors automatically locked! Frustrated and helpless, I stood outside in the blizzard watching the car, running and in gear, spin deeper into the drift. The car heater continued to fill the car with warm air. The windshield wipers kept the windshield free from snow. The driver's seat was tilted comfortably; the radio played relaxing music. There I stood, shivering outside in the snow, without the keys! All the comforts and conveniences of the vehicle were absolutely worthless to me. Without the keys, I had no access to them.

Sadly, I know Christians who struggle through life without realizing they do have access to God and all His resources for a victorious and abundant life. Jesus repeatedly said, "Don't worry!" Why? Because He knew the King. He knew His Father's love, mercy, grace, faithfulness, forgiveness, and kindness and He knew it was senseless to worry when God had made such bountiful provision for citizens of His kingdom. Yet we still worry about exams, health, assignments, finances, friendships, the future, job security, parents, and a thousand other things! Our concerns may be real, but we can miss the important truth that God stands ready to meet the needs of His children.

KEYS OF THE KINGDOM
Read Matthew 16:19.

What do you think Jesus meant by keys of the kingdom?

What are you to do with them? How do you do this?

Suppose a wealthy man adopted an impoverished orphan as his son. Imagine that the benevolent man took the boy to his mansion and showed him through every luxurious room. In each room were different treasures. At the end of the tour, the man handed his new son a set of keys and said, "These keys will open any door in this house. If there is anything you or your friends ever need, help yourself!"

In Matthew 16:19 Jesus was telling His disciples that because of their special relationship with the Father, they were being given a set of keys. As children of God, they now had direct access to God and to His resources.

GOD'S PROMISES TO KINGDOM CITIZENS
Read carefully the wonderful promises made to kingdom citizens in the following Scripture.

> **"God is able to make all grace abound to you, so that in all things at all times, having all that you need, you will abound in every good work"** **(2 Corinthians 9:8).**

> **"I can do everything through him who gives me strength"(Philippians 4:13).**

> **"My God will meet all your needs according to his glorious riches in Christ Jesus" (Philippians 4:19).**

State these verses in terms of your current life situation.

2 Corinthians 9:8

Philippians 4:13

Philippians 4:19

These are encouraging promises. They are invitations extended to Christians. God wants us to seek Him and His provisions. Remember what it cost God to provide these resources. It cost Him His Son. Will you accept His invitation to rely on Him for all your needs?

GOD'S PROMISES ARE GIVEN TO GLORIFY HIMSELF,
NOT TO SATISFY OUR EVERY WISH.

A word of caution here. God's promises are given to glorify Himself, not to satisfy our every wish. Don't be like the preschooler who was frustrated because his parents would not allow him to do what he asked. In frustrated defiance he shouted, "I can do everything through Him who gives me strength" (Philippians 4:13). This little boy's Scripture memory was commendable; his theology was a bit off!

Scripture holds a great number of promises for God's children. List additional promises of God that have been particularly meaningful to you. Give scriptural references if possible.

Promise 1:

Promise 2:

Promise 3:

Promise 4:

Promise 5:

On a Sunday morning in October 1995, a 5-year-old boy and his 3-year-old sister from Brossard, Quebec, couldn't wait for their parents to wake up and feed them breakfast. So, snatching the keys to the family van, they drove almost a mile to McDonald's! The little boy virtually had to lie down to reach the gas pedal, occasionally popping up to see where he was going! A cashier at the gas station next door to McDonald's was taken aback when she saw a "driverless" van approach. Then, to her amazement, the door opened and two small children in pajamas and bare feet climbed out. The young boy later told police, "I had my seat belt on, and so did my sister. I'm not going to go to prison."[1]

Those two children discovered that the keys gave them access to something much bigger and more powerful than themselves. So it is for the Christian. By ourselves we're weak, but we hold the keys to God's bountiful kingdom. It may be that you grew up in a home where you were not affirmed and love was not expressed. Even as a Christian you may long to experience love. It would be tragic for you to go through life longing to be loved when you hold the keys to God's promises such as Romans 8:35-38, which says that nothing can separate you from God's love. Or, perhaps you're a Christian who has fallen into sin. You may feel terrible about your failure and fear that God would never relate to someone so prone to sin. It would be futile for you to live a defeated life when 1 John 1:9 promises that if you confess your sins, God is faithful to forgive you and to cleanse you, making you pure in His sight. Promises like these and many others are yours if you will accept them as God's invitation to you.

When Jesus gave the keys of the kingdom to His disciples, they came with a responsibility. That is, the disciples' special relationship with the heavenly Father and their access to His resources was not to be hoarded. Just as they knew God, the disciples could invite others to establish this same relationship with Him. Thus God's provisions would be accessible to them also. For example, you might have a friend who's depressed and discouraged. You may not have wise words to share or power to change his circumstances, yet you have the "keys of the kingdom." You have access to Philippians 4:6-7, which promises that if we take our cares to God, His peace, which surpasses comprehension, will surround our hearts and minds until we're no longer anxious, even in the most difficult circumstances. It's not your answers people need, nor your peace, nor your resources. People need God and what only He can give. You have been given the keys to God's storehouse and can guide people to God so they can receive His provision for their problems.

Think of three people you know who are experiencing a need. List those people in the space below and indicate their specific need.

Now look back over the list and write a Scripture that addresses each need you have listed.

Commit yourself to do the following.

First, tell your friends of the scriptural promise God has given that can be theirs if they will accept it in faith.

Second, begin praying that these Scriptures will become real and personal to your friends. When you look at the magnificent ways people like the apostle Paul prayed for others in Ephesians 1:15-23; 3:14-21; and Colossians 1:9-12, it's hard to pray anything more uplifting for people than this. You have the keys to these promises. Commit to pray them for others and watch to see how God implements these promises into their lives.

What did God say to you during your study today?

What will you do as a result?

THE KINGDOM'S IMPLICATIONS

> "If anyone comes to me and does not hate his father and mother, his wife and children, his brothers and sisters—yes, even his own life—he cannot be my disciple. And anyone who does not carry his cross and follow me cannot be my disciple" (Luke 14:26-27).

It's amazing how far some people will go to gain notoriety! They devote their entire lives to pursuing fame. For example, one man placed two cables in his mouth and held two Cessna aircraft for three seconds with the engines running at 2,400 rpm and a combined horsepower of 310. Why? To claim a world record, of course! Another man collected 2,561 different brands of chewing gum to set a record. Did you know that the longest single apple peel is 52.51 meters? And were you aware that the fastest noodle maker can make 4,096 noodles in 58.2 seconds? The world's greatest yo-yoer can do 21,633 yo-yo tricks in three hours. When interviewed, this man said, not surprisingly, "yo-yo is my life." Sadly, some people devote their lives to trivial, eternally inconsequential pursuits.

There are many purposes to which one could devote one's life. Some are more noble than others. In each case, a person must decide how serious they will be about their commitment.

When Jesus stood on the seashore and invited John to follow Him, John had no idea what this would involve. John released his life to Jesus, not knowing what it would cost, where he might have to travel, or what might be asked of him. He had come face to face with God's Son and he knew it was an invitation he must accept. As a result, John experienced life with dimensions beyond his wildest dreams. He walked with the Son of God. He witnessed Jesus performing miracles. He saw God raise people from the dead. He wrote several books of holy Scripture. He cared for the mother of the Son of God. His life influenced millions of people over the ensuing centuries. John accepted God's invitation to live as a child of God in the kingdom of the Son of God (Colossians 1:13).

Jesus invited His followers to consider the implications of belonging to God's kingdom.

1. KINGDOM BEFORE FAMILY
Read Luke 14:26-27.

How did Jesus say your relationships with others should compare to your relationship with Him?

What does this mean you should do if you ever face a choice between pleasing your family and pleasing Jesus?

Have you ever had to choose between the wishes of your family members and obeying God? Write an example.

Perhaps the most difficult invitations you ever will receive from God are those requiring you to do things to which your family objects. We've seen many young adults weep as they agonized over the alienation they were experiencing from their parents because they had been baptized, or had committed their life to missions, or had witnessed to their siblings. We once had two university students arrive at our home on Christmas Day. They had been told to leave their parents' home because they had been talking about the Lord. In the years that followed they sought to honor their parents, treating them with respect, while remaining obedient to God's direction.

2. KINGDOM AFTER COUNTING THE COST
Read the following verses, and then answer the questions.

"Suppose one of you wants to build a tower. Will he not first sit down and estimate the cost to see if he has enough money to complete it? For if he lays the foundation and is not able to finish it, everyone who sees it will ridicule him, saying, 'This fellow began to build and was not able to finish.' Or suppose a king is about to go to war against another king. Will he not first sit down and consider whether he is able with ten thousand men to oppose the one coming against him with twenty thousand? If he is not able, he will send a delegation while the other is still a long way off and will ask for terms of peace" (Luke 14:28-32).

What is the truth found in this passage?

Why is it important to count the cost before following Jesus?

Jesus cautioned, "You must count the cost if you are to follow Me." Make no mistake; following Jesus will cost you! If you try to live the Christian life unaware that Jesus expects absolute obedience to everything He tells you to do, you may reach a point in your Christian faith where you are unwilling go further. If you "count the cost" of your commitment to Christ, then God's work in you will not be incomplete or abandoned when the going gets tough. Remember, the cost of not following Jesus is always far greater!

HE SHOULD HAVE COUNTED THE COST!

When I (Richard) took my future wife, Lisa, on one of our first dates, I wanted to impress her. I took her to one of the nicest restaurants in the city and offered to treat her to anything on the menu. Unfortunately, I hadn't accurately counted the cost. Lisa ordered a steak dinner with all the trimmings! And dessert! When the bill came, I panicked. I was $10 short. Suddenly, I remembered that the ashtray in my jalopy held my parking-meter money. Calmly, I excused myself and walked to the door, where I flew outside to my car. Removing the full ashtray, I stuffed it under my jacket and returned to the restaurant.

Red-faced, I then confessed my quandary to Lisa. Laughing, she took the ashtray to the drugstore next door and had the mound of change converted into dollar bills. There was just enough! Chagrined, I paid the bill and meekly left the restaurant, determined that next time I'd count the cost (or carry a credit card)!

Sadly, we've seen Christians who did not count the cost before embarking on their Christian pilgrimage. Their motive for accepting Christ was to ensure a place in heaven when they died. They wanted to be eligible for a wide assortment of blessings, but wanted only minimal obligations. Then God began to exercise His lordship over their lives. Suddenly there was a cost involved. Perhaps it was their prejudicial attitudes He wanted to change. Or maybe God asked them to leave their large, comfortable church to join a mission work in the downtown area. God might have asked them to take a job overseas, where they could be a support to the missionaries in that country. They realized there was much more required of them than they had bargained for. Rather than being transformed into an effective servant of God, they became spiritually stagnant and of no use to God. How much easier it would have been for them if they'd entered God's kingdom prepared to pay the price.

Do you think you clearly understand what God expects of you as a Christian? Are you prepared to make the kind of commitment His lordship requires? Explain.

3. THE KINGDOM BEFORE POSSESSIONS
Read Luke 14:33.

Write the truth of this verse in terms of your life and obedience to God.

Jesus said that if your response to God's invitation comes into conflict with your commitment to material possessions and ambitions, there should be no question what you should do. He was saying that your possessions should have no hold upon your life. You ought to be able to part with everything God asks of you. If you possess anything that hinders you from being on mission with God, get rid of it! One young couple heard about mission work in a foreign country and became concerned about the needs of the missionaries. This couple had limited financial resources, but they believed God was inviting them to get involved with Him in this work. They canceled their cable TV service and sent the money to the mission field.

> JESUS SAID THAT IF YOUR RESPONSE TO GOD'S INVITATION
> COMES INTO CONFLICT WITH YOUR COMMITMENT
> TO MATERIAL POSSESSIONS AND AMBITIONS,
> THERE SHOULD BE NO QUESTION WHAT YOU SHOULD DO.

Do you have possessions or financial commitments that prevent you from doing all God wants you to do? Pray and ask God to reveal anything that hinders you from doing His will. Write down what He tells you and then release those things to Him.

As you search your heart, would you be willing to go anywhere God might ask you to go? If not, where are you unwilling to go?

What do you sense God wants to do in and through your life right now? Are you willing for Him to do this work in you?

What did God say to you during your study today?

What will you do as a result?

THE KINGDOM'S POWER

> "You will receive power when the Holy Spirit comes on you; and you will be my witnesses in Jerusalem, and in all Judea and Samaria, and to the ends of the earth" (Acts 1:8).

As a college student, Dennis responded to God's invitation to serve in summer missions in the Philippines. One of the activities Dennis enjoyed was playing basketball with the young people. Dennis was a 5-foot, 8-inch African-American. Many of the Filipinos had never seen an American, and fewer had seen an African-American. As he played basketball, Filipinos would gather around the court to watch, thinking he actually was a professional basketball player. One day, an elderly man approached Dennis and asked him to go with him to tell his village about Jesus. Dennis readily agreed. Once he had committed to go, he was startled to hear that the last missionary who had gone to this village had been killed by communist guerrillas. After some hesitation Dennis went, albeit fearfully. The first people he shared Jesus with accepted Christ as their Lord and Savior. Dennis was jubilant, but as he left their house he came face to face with communist guerrillas holding machine guns. Praying for God's strength, he carefully approached the men. Their leader stepped forward and asked, "Are you a missionary?"

"Yes," he replied.

"Did you tell about Jesus in that house?"

"Yes."

Then the soldier smiled, "We read about you. You come out of retirement. You score 50 points against the Knicks." Then he turned to his fellow soldiers and exclaimed, "It's Michael Jordan!" Dennis was relieved and amused that he could have been mistaken for one of the most famous basketball players in the world! As he returned to the United States, he carried with him the thrill of having experienced God's protection and knowing God had used him to impact a village on the other side of the world.

Jesus wants you to be a world Christian. Notice His invitation in Acts 1:8:

What did Jesus promise His followers?

What did He instruct His followers to do?

Jesus gave this incredible invitation to His timid disciples to touch and change their world. He said they would receive *power*. This is the Greek word from which we get the word *dynamite*. Jesus said their power would not be inherent to themselves, but would come from the presence of the Holy Spirit in their lives. The Holy Spirit's role is to guide, equip, and empower the people of God to be instruments for God's redemptive purposes. They would begin in Jerusalem, the center of Jewish religion. They would go to Judea, the rural and less-traveled areas of the nation. They would go still farther afield into Samaria. This was an area not too distant in miles but culturally on the other side of the world. The Spirit would have to remove the disciples' prejudices and fears for them to reach the people in Samaria. Finally, the Spirit would take them to the ends of the earth. They had a narrow view of their world. All the nations but theirs were considered unclean. Yet Jesus was saying God wanted to evangelize the world through them.

What does it mean for the Holy Spirit's presence and power to guide you?

How is the Spirit guiding you to share God's full provision for life with others?

SERVING GOD IN MEXICO

Twenty-five young adults from Louisiana sensed God inviting them to minister at a Christian encampment in Acuna, Mexico. Raising the necessary funds and working out all the details of the trip had been a challenge, yet God had provided for all their needs. At the end of each day, they gathered to worship. One evening as Mario, a laborer, was hurrying home from a long day's work, he cut through the encampment to save time. As he walked alone in the darkness, he heard singing coming from a house nearby. Curious, he climbed on top of a wall for a better view. One of the young adults noticed Mario and invited him to join them. That night Mario became a child of God. The group who had sacrificially traveled from Louisiana to Mexico came to understand that God's kingdom extended far beyond their community.

How can God use you and your friends to reach your community?

Do you have the world in your heart? One of the best-known Scripture verses says, "God so loved the world that He gave His one and only Son" (John 3:16). Do you love the world the way God does? God loved it so much, He gave the One He loved the most, His Son, to redeem it.

Take the following test to see how much of the world is in your heart.

I keep informed of world events.
❏ Never ❏ Sometimes ❏ Regularly

I pray for the people in other countries.
❏ Never ❏ Sometimes ❏ Regularly

I pray specifically for world crises.
❏ Never ❏ Sometimes ❏ Regularly

I pray for missionaries around the world.
❏ Never ❏ Sometimes ❏ Regularly

I read mission magazines and books.
❏ Never ❏ Sometimes ❏ Regularly

I have served in short-term missions.
❏ Never ❏ Sometimes ❏ Regularly

I give money to international mission causes.   I attend missions meetings.
❏ Never ❏ Sometimes ❏ Regularly   ❏ Never ❏ Sometimes ❏ Regularly

I befriend people from other countries.   I pay attention to foreign news.
❏ Never ❏ Sometimes ❏ Regularly   ❏ Never ❏ Sometimes ❏ Regularly

How did you do? What could you do to increase your involvement in world missions and causes?

JESUS GAVE AN INCREDIBLE INVITATION
TO HIS TIMID DISCIPLES TO TOUCH AND CHANGE
THEIR WORLD. HE SAID THEY WOULD RECEIVE POWER
NOT INHERENT TO THEMSELVES, BUT FROM
THE PRESENCE OF THE HOLY SPIRIT IN THEIR LIVES.

We're always disappointed when we find Christians who are unconcerned with what's happening in the world. They don't watch the international news or read about world events. They know little about missions. They don't know the heart of God for the people of the world. They don't give to support missions nor do they pray for missionaries. Yet Jesus clearly commanded us to be world Christians.

Would you call yourself a world Christian? Do others see you as a world Christian?

BRICKLAYING FOR GOD
In the summer of 1995, the Canadian Southern Baptist Seminary in Cochrane, Alberta, appealed for help to build a new classroom building. The school had no resources, and they prayed that God would provide laborers for this project. A small church in Texas heard their request.

In their church was a bricklayer. His father and son, also both bricklayers, were members of the church as well. When they heard that the seminary needed to lay 50,000 bricks, they volunteered to go. Then the pastor agreed to go and run the forklift. Teenagers said they were willing to mix the mortar. Senior adults offered to build and load scaffolding. Women volunteered to cook the meals. They formed a work team of 20 and headed to Canada. Their work day began at 5:30 a.m., with their first break at 7:00 a.m. for breakfast. The crew did a magnificent job, providing a strong Christian witness to the entire community. As word spread of their sacrificial efforts, requests began to come from all over the world where bricklayers were needed to construct buildings for Christian causes. Now that little church has more offers than they know what to do with! One church, willing and prepared to respond to God's invitation, is impacting their world for Christ.

What is God building into your life that He might use to impact your world?

How is the world being changed because of you?

What did God say to you during your study today?

What will you do as a result?

THE KINGDOM'S ACCOUNTING

> "We make it our goal to please him, whether we are at home in the body
> or away from it. For we must all appear before the judgment seat of
> Christ, that each one may receive what is due him for the things done
> while in the body, whether good or bad" (2 Corinthians 5:9-10).

Once a man approached me (Henry) at the close of a conference. He shared how as a
young boy he had sensed God leading him to become a doctor in order to serve on
the mission field. He had entered medicine, specializing in the immune system. After
graduation he accepted a position in research at a major university. He married and
was active in his church. However, he realized that God's invitation, given so many years
earlier, still stood. Now he had to decide how to respond. He realized he would have to
give an account for how he responded. A year later I rejoiced to hear that he had been
appointed to Uganda as a medical missionary! He had accepted God's invitation and
was touching the world with his critical knowledge and skill in AIDS research.

The apostle Paul was daily motivated by a keen awareness that his life, at all times, must
please God.

Read 2 Corinthians 5:9-10.

What was a major motivating factor affecting Paul's life?

What does it mean to be accountable to God?

Paul was one of the greatest saints of all time. He shared life-transforming messages,
started churches, wrote letters that became Scripture, and developed the church's

theology. Scripture reveals that the motivating principle behind all he did was the knowledge of Christ's love and that every person would have to give an account of his actions before a holy and just God. We tend to think judgment is reserved for nonbelievers. Yet, Paul said he knew the fear of the Lord. Paul had a reverent concern that he would never have to stand ashamed before his Savior.

How do you feel about one day standing before God and giving an account of your actions, both good and bad?

Do you have a reverent fear of God? What is the evidence of this?

Notice in this Scripture how Paul said you could evaluate the things you do in this life.

> "His work will be shown for what it is, because the Day will bring it to light. It will be revealed with fire, and the fire will test the quality of each man's work. If what he has built survives, he will receive his reward. If it is burned up, he will suffer loss; he himself will be saved, but only as one escaping through the flames" (1 Corinthians 3:13-15).

What will happen to the things you invest in during your life?

Is it possible to do nothing of eternal value and still enter heaven? How?

What kind of works will last in heaven?

Paul wanted no disappointments at the end of his life, so he left nothing to chance. He knew full well that it was possible to live as a Christian and have nothing to show for it when his life was over. Paul used the vivid imagery of fire cleansing and burning away impurities. He said God's judgment would be like a fire that burned away every sinful act. When every sin is removed, whatever's left will be acceptable to God.

What activities are you involved in that would survive God's cleansing fires?

Do you have thoughts, attitudes, habits, or sins that you know would not meet God's standards in judgment? How could you deal with them now?

How are you investing your life wisely?

AN EXPANDED VISION

John was a successful college minister who worked faithfully on his campus. He began to feel an intensifying burden to establish new campus ministries at major universities around the world. He traveled with his students to a foreign university and found that young adults there were responsive to the gospel message. He felt impressed to take students from his campus to visit the major universities throughout the former Soviet Union. To his surprise, the people were not only receptive to the gospel message but urged him to return. John eventually felt God leading him to resign his campus job and to devote himself full-time to working at universities around the world.

CONCLUSION

Today there are thousands of young adults who are responding to God's invitation to be on mission with Him. This may be the generation that sees more college students and twenty-somethings involved in missions throughout North America and the world than any other time in history. Young adults responding to God's invitation are taking the gospel to the inner cities of America, to prisons, to hospitals for the dying, to the political offices of Washington, D.C., to other world capitals, to professional sports teams, and to the military. Young Christians are realizing God has far more for them than they could have imagined as they impact the world like never before.

During this study, you've been challenged to respond to God's invitation. Look back through your notes and write in the space below everything you committed to God.

Take a moment to pray about each one.

Whom have you asked to hold you accountable to the commitments you have made? List their names.

As you come to the end of this study, what's the one thing you know you must do as a result of what God is saying to you?

Do you need to make any of your decisions public in your church or Christian organization? If so, when will you do this?

Are you keeping a record of all God has invited you to do and your corresponding obedience? If not, make a list of the following.

What God invited you to do:

The date He spoke to you:

Your response:

We pray that you will take seriously God's invitation to you. We have both experienced God's invitation and realize the incredible joy of being used to influence the world for Christ. We sincerely want you to have this experience too. How will *you* respond to God's invitation? God's invitation is your greatest challenge!

Now that you've completed this study, are there areas you've identified that you need to understand more fully? Go back and review that material. You have the tools to guide you. Keep them for the rest of your life.

THE FIVE REALITIES OF EXPERIENCING GOD

1. God is always at work around you.
2. God loves you and invites you to become involved with Him in His work.
3. God speaks to you by His Holy Spirit through the Bible, prayer, circumstances, and the church.
4. God's invitation will create a crisis of belief, requiring you to make adjustments in your life.
5. When you obey, you experience God's power working through you, and you bring Him glory.

NOTES

SESSION 1

1. Mrs. Howard Taylor, *Borden of Yale: The Life That Counts* (Philadelphia: China Inland Mission, 1926).

SESSION 2

1. Phillips Brooks, *Twenty Sermons* (1923), 330.
2. L. R. Scarborough, *With Christ After the Lost* (1923), 82.

SESSION 3

1. Pierre Berton, *My Country: The Remarkable Past* (Toronto: McClelland and Stewart, 1976), 272–85.
2. John Pollock, *The Cambridge Seven* (London: Inter-Varsity, 1955), 111.

SESSION 4

1. *Winnipeg Free Press,* "Inquest told of 'heroic' bid to save pals," November 27, 1991, A5.
2. Corrie Ten Boom, *The Hiding Place* (Grand Rapids, MI: Chosen Books, 1984), 247–48.

SESSION 5

1. Kenneth W. Osbeck, *101 Hymn Stories* (Grand Rapids: Kregel Publications, 1982), 127.
2. "Thank You for the Beating," *Christian Herald,* April 1988.
3. "Dietrich Bonhoeffer," *Christian History* 10, no. 4.
4. Ten Boom, *The Hiding Place,* 210–20.

SESSION 6

1. "Persecution in the Early Church," *Christian History* 9, no. 3: 33.
2. Leslie K. Tarr, "A Prayer Meeting that Lasted 100 Years," *Christian History* 1, no. 1: 18.

SESSION 7

1. "Tot takes sister for breakfast in family van," *Calgary Herald,* October 12, 1995.

EXPERIENCING GOD: YOUNG ADULTS

WELCOME to *Experiencing God: God's Invitation to Young Adults* leader guide. This leader guide is designed to provide you, the leader, with the foundation you need to lead your group through an effective, engaging, and meaningful Bible study.

As group leader, you have the unique responsibility to set the tone for your group and guide each gathering's conversation. As you spend time with your group, pray with them and serve them in unexpected ways. When you lay that foundation of trust and belonging, you enable God to transform the lives of your group members.

You'll find study notes, commentaries, articles, word studies, and other resources to supplement your preparation at mywsb.com.

BEFORE YOUR FIRST GATHERING

❏ Read the *Experiencing God: God's Invitation to Young Adults* Bible study book.

❏ Read through the leader guide to familiarize yourself with the group session format.

❏ Post study information on your church's website, in the church bulletin, or on your personal blog or social-network page.

❏ Distribute a Bible study book to each person in your group.

INTRO TO THE LEADER

Think to yourself for a moment what you want to get out of this Bible study. This series is about, as the title says, experiencing God specifically on the young adult level. As young adults, the audience in front of you is facing a unique and specific set of choices, circumstances, and scenarios that no other life group is facing. Being a Christian as a young adult can be very different than being a Christian in a youth group or anything young adults have experienced before in life.

Your role is not to lecture or impart new materials but to lead your group to discuss what they've learned during the week and what they've committed themselves to do in response.

Leader tip. If your group feels that God is speaking to them and they need more time to process what He is saying, they may choose to use two weeks to cover each session in order to better understand and respond to Him.

QUESTIONS & DISCUSSION

To help you facilitate the group, suggested questions and statements for you to make will guide your group experience. The study itself contains supplemental questions to further enhance group learning. Be sure to read both the Bible study book and the leader guide prior to each session to best prepare each group time.

DURING YOUR FIRST SESSION

Begin by praying, asking God to bless you and your time together with your group, not just today, or the first time you gather, but in all of your meetings together. Pray specifically for openness and honesty in all of your discussions and conversations as well as for God to open all the hearts in the group to God's invitation to live out His will in each life. Start each gathering of this Bible study with this practice and these thoughts in mind.

Before diving into the first lesson, lead a discussion on the challenges, or maybe the ease, of being a Christian as a young adult in your world today. Adapt the following questions according to the needs of your group.

How is being a Christian on a college campus or in the workplace different from being a Christian as a child or in a youth group?

What are some of the unique challenges that you face in your life as a Christian right now?

How are you living out your faith on a daily basis?

What are you doing actively to further your relationship with Christ?

How are you controlling your level of commitment without a parent or guardian guiding you in your faith?

Finally, preface this study by telling the group of young adults to prepare themselves for seven weeks of refinement.

This is a study that's not only good for opening the doors to deepening a relationship with Jesus Christ, but it's also a very good way to refine your relationship with Jesus. The prayer for your group is that they will whittle away the distractions surrounding them, and allow themselves to focus fully on Christ—not just when you meet together as a group, but in every minute of every day.

SEEING LIFE FROM GOD'S PERSPECTIVE

OPENING

Welcome each person to the group. Spend a few moments getting to know one another. Then begin the session.

The first of five realities underlying this *Experiencing God* study that we need to explore is that God speaks to us by His Holy Spirit through the Bible, prayer, circumstances, and the church. Keep this reality in mind as you begin.

Lead your group in a time of prayer, thanking God for bringing them together. Acknowledge God's presence in the group and ask the Holy Spirit to be your teacher during the session. Ask God to begin bonding the lives of each person in the group together in Christian love and accountability.

DISCUSSION

Point out the quote of George Bernard Shaw on page 13 when he replied, "I would be the man George Bernard Shaw could have been, but never was."

Lead the group to discuss these questions:

What are the things you can do that will really matter in life?

How can you discover the person God intends you to be?

Call on a volunteer to summarize the illustration of William Borden's life. Remind your group of his statement to his mother:

> "When I look ahead a few years, it seems as though the only thing to do is to prepare for the foreign field" (p. 14).

What would you do if you had the same amount of money William had?

Encourage the group to be honest, not giving the typical "church" answer.

In what ways do we naturally assume the wealthy are more valuable because they can give more?

Do you believe God can use people more or less depending on their wealth? Explain.

Most of us in this room are not millionaires as William Borden was. In fact, a lot of us in the room would identify at the other end of the financial spectrum: *I don't have any money for missions; I'm trying to pay rent; I have student loans; and so forth.*

Many in the Bible had no resources and they were able to accomplish much for God's glory.

What biblical examples do we have of rich and poor people who God used for great things?

What are some things you're doing now or would like to do to advance the gospel?

You may not have the money to buy an orphanage or fly halfway around the world, but you do have a city, campus, or work place where you can influence the world for Christ.

How do you imagine your life five years from now?

Refer to page 16 and the concerns about the future that they checked. (If young adults haven't previously completed this response activity, allow them a few minutes to do so.)

How can God's knowledge of your future affect the way He leads you?

How are you currently investing in the future?

It's important to be aware and to remember that God knows everything. He knows your plan and He knows His. From the beginning to the end, He knows it all. He is actively at work everywhere. Read Jonah 1–3.

Compare and contrast God's plan for Jonah with Jonah's plan for himself.

How did Jonah's plan work out (1:15,17)?

How did God's plan work out (3:2-3a)?

Just because we may think we can duck under the radar and hide from God doesn't mean we can. Jonah didn't like God's plan and tried to live his life on his own.

Describe a time when you knew God specifically told you to do something. Did you try to run like Jonah? Did you say yes? What happened?

Like it or not, God knows you. He knows what you've done and what you're going to do. God exists in our past, present, and future. Take a minute to discuss your future plans. (Allow discussion time.)

Chances are most spouted off a checklist: graduate, travel, find a career, get married, buy a house, get a pet, have kids, retire.

How will you respond if God's plan for you is different than your own? Will you choose to follow?

How do we know God's plan for us? What role does the Holy Spirit have in this process?

What's one thing you've heard God saying to you recently as you've read the Bible? How have you acted on it?

What's one thing you've heard God saying to you through prayer? How have you acted on it?

What's one thing you've heard God speaking to you through a circumstance? How have you acted on it?

What's one thing you've heard God speaking to you through another person? How have you acted on it?

Refer to page 33 and ask your group to note the boxes they checked regarding their relationships with God. Direct them to form pairs and to share with each other two actions they have identified that will enhance their relationships with God.

Lead the group to compare the investments lists of Jesus and the rich fool. (See p. 38.) Call on volunteers to share their answers to the first three questions from page 39:

What's one way you're tempted to invest your life in temporal rather than eternal things?

How could this keep you from experiencing God's best?

What changes do you need to make in the way you're investing your life?

CLOSING

Give each person an index card. Instruct them to write *God's Perspective* and then list ways their perspective on life has been changed during this study.

What changes do you plan to make in your life so that you view life through God's perspective?

Lead in a time of prayer and dismiss.

OPTIONAL VIDEO

While your group is going through this study, schedule time to watch the hour-long *Experiencing God* documentary, available at LifeWay.com. This film explores how God has placed *Experiencing God* in the hands of international leaders, prisoners, and Christ followers who have been awakened to realize the world how God sees the world.

CHARACTER: THE BASIS FOR YOUR FUTURE

OPENING

Arrange the chairs in pairs or threes. Write the following review questions on the board or on sheets of paper to distribute.

What three things greatly affect your character?

You will give the majority of your _____, _____, and energy to those things that are most important to you.

The most important thing in my life for which God looks is: (Check all that apply.)

❏ My ability   ❏ My faithfulness
❏ My resources   ❏ My availability
❏ My personality   ❏ My character

True or False

___ Nothing can separate me from the love of God.
___ God's assignment and His love for me will never change.
___ God loves me and doesn't expect me to change.
___ There are no shortcuts to character.
___ What happens around me should determine how I act.

As the group arrives, invite them to complete the quiz. Once everyone has had time to finish, instruct the pairs or threes to discuss their answers with each other. Instruct each group to appoint one person to lead the group in prayer, calling on God's leadership in today's session.

DISCUSSION

Call on a volunteer to explain why God matches assignments with character.

What is character? How does God use our circumstances to help grow and develop our character?

As we learned from our reading this week, "Character dictates conduct. ... This is where you make moral decisions and hold your values" (p. 43).

What are some of your values?

Do you consider these values to be biblically based or culturally defined? Is it wrong to value these things? Explain.

Ask a volunteer to read 1 Corinthians 6:19.

Our bodies are temples; therefore, we should treat them well. If we desire to honor and respect the body God has given us, what we put into and how we use our bodies should reflect Christ.

How can you apply this line of thinking to some other values brought up or listed?

Why is character important to God?

Enlist a volunteer to read Luke 6:43-45.

What's one way to evaluate a person's character?

We can evaluate a person's character by the fruit produced from his or her life. Call on a volunteer to read Galatians 5:22-23.

These ideas of love, joy, and peace not only guide our lives, but they also reveal to us what we value. As young adults, consciously or not, you will develop a value system that will stick with you for the rest of your life. At times, these values may be seen as radical ideas—not drinking at a party, not going too far with a boyfriend or girlfriend, or not lying to your boss as to why you were late … again.

When was a time where your values in Christ influenced your decisions more than those around you?

What distracts you from sticking to these values?

Believe it or not, your peers are your number one influence. Regardless of whether you know them or just see them in passing, people, social media, and marketing all heavily influence your decisions.

What worldly influences have you grabbed onto in your life—from simpler things like fashion trends and electronics to more difficult life decisions?

Outside influences aren't necessarily bad, but they can lead to destructive habits. Giving in to the smallest thing can lead down a path of destruction.

Think to yourself about a situation you or a friend were in where one thing led to another and, when it was all said and done, a self-destructive habit was born. Share as you feel comfortable.

Was there any redemption? Have you or this friend found the saving grace that you needed?

Maybe you or your friend are still in need of redemption. Highlight the story of King David, described as a man after God's own heart. But did you know he was also an adulterer, a murderer, and a liar? Did you know God still continued to use him in incredible ways after he committed these sins?

Much like David, there's nothing that can separate you from the love of God as long as you experience His redemption.

Let's shift now to focus more on the heart. Ask a volunteer to read Matthew 6:19-21.

What's the difference between "treasures on earth" (v. 19) and "treasures in heaven" (v. 20)?

How can you better focus on "treasures in heaven"?

What are you doing to develop godly character in your life?

Instruct the pairs to list things that create a divided heart in a person's life. Call on them to share their lists. Record their responses on a large sheet of paper or board. Lead the group to list ways that they can develop an undivided heart. Call on volunteers to share what items they checked on pages 56–57. Guide the group to discuss their answers to the questions from page 58:

After evaluating the use of your time, what adjustments do you think God wants to make?

What's God saying to you about your habits?

Call on a volunteer to read Matthew 25:21.

What was the basis of the master's praise of his servant?

What effect did the servant's faithfulness have on his master?

What responsibilities or tasks has God assigned you? What does the size of the responsibility imply about your level of faithfulness to God?

Refer to the faithfulness exam on pages 61–62. Call on volunteers to share what the exam revealed to them about their faithfulness to God.

Based on this week's study, what's one lesson you can learn from your failure?

Divide the group into three teams and assign each team one of the character studies on failure ("David the Murderer," "Peter the Denier," and "Thomas the Doubter") on pages 64–65. Instruct the teams to list the biblical principals about failure they learned from the three men. Call on teams to report. Encourage the group to share one area of failure for which everyone can pray during the week.

CLOSING

Invite the group to share their answers to the last two questions on page 67.

Arrange the group into pairs or threes for a time of prayer. Then dismiss.

CAREER: A VEHICLE FOR GOD'S PURPOSES

OPENING

Arrange the chairs in pairs or threes. Write the following review questions on a board or on sheets of paper. As group members arrive, invite them to begin answering the review questions in small groups.

What are ways to discover God's will as revealed by the Holy Spirit?

What's one thing that spoke to you during this week's study?

Allowing time for everyone to finish, ask groups to appoint one person in each group to lead them in prayer, calling on God's leadership in today's session. Then come back together as a large group.

DISCUSSION

Refer to the "Introduction" on page 69.

Describe someone who has made a difference in your life.

What evidence would you cite to demonstrate your life has made a difference to someone else?

Be sensitive to young adults who may feel discouraged about their lives regarding this question.

Discuss the comments under "God Has a Plan" (p. 74) to encourage the group about God's plan for their future.

What's the difference between being called to a relationship and being called to a vocation?

Refer to "Career or Relationship?" (p. 72). Lead the group to discuss their answers to the first two questions on the bottom of page 71:

How has God begun to show you ways He might use you in a vocation to make a difference for His kingdom?

Are you willing to obey the next thing God tells you even if you cannot see what God has in mind for your future? What fears and/or dreams do you need to let go of in order to follow God's plan for you?

Ask everyone to go back into pairs or threes. Instruct them to discuss their answers to the following questions.

Can you please God while struggling to believe Him? Explain your response.

How will you respond when your life circumstances require trusting Him?

After a few minutes come back into one large group. Ask:

If you aren't called to professional ministry, how can you use a "secular" calling for His purposes and His glory?

If you don't yet know God's purposes for your career, does that mean you've missed your calling? Explain.

These are questions that young adults ask all the time. Here is the simple answer to that last question: Through a personal relationship with Jesus Christ, He will lead you down the path for His purposes. Regardless of what your profession is or will be, God will show you exactly how you are to be used in it.

Much like Joseph from your reading this past week, the path God calls you to will likely have many twists and turns. Your journey as a student or young professional might be to reach out to a nonbeliever on your campus or place of work. It might be to start a Bible study. It might be to read your Bible in the same spot every day and hope someone stops and asks questions. God knows how to maximize each day of your life.

Is it easy to trust this idea? Why or why not?

Scripture tells us that even before the creation of the earth, God knew us.

What allows you to walk with God down this path?

What's the difference between faith and belief? Why is it important to make this distinction?

Read James 2:19.

Belief is based on what we know to be true. The demons that James described saw Jesus. They knew beyond a shadow of a doubt that He was and is real. He existed; they had a genuine knowledge of Him.

Read Hebrews 11:1-4.

Faith is a core value. It's a condition of the heart, not just of the mind. It's something that's unwavering. Faith allowed Jonah to survive in the fish. Faith caused Joseph to stay with Mary even after suffering. Faith allowed Moses to free his entire people even with the Egyptian army against him.

It's faith that leads and guides us down life's path. The beautiful part of this is that God is leading the entire way. We're not walking through darkness, but rather God is leading us through a path of light.

What are you doing to make sure you are staying on the correct path?

Call on volunteers to share the "Biblical Truths" they recorded on page 78. Review the five truths the Blackaby's noticed in the verses (pp. 78–79).

Based on these truths, what adjustments do you need to make in your life?

Read the following statement.

"Circumstances alone can be confusing and must be evaluated in light of what the Spirit also says to you through the Bible, prayer, and the church" (p. 82).

Share an experience from your own life when you discovered that circumstances can be confusing when viewed without listening to God's voice.

God reveals His plans for us through many different ways—specific Scriptures, prayer, circumstances, and even other people.

Regardless of how He speaks to you, are you listening to what He says? How do you hear Him speak?

God does not hold back on communicating with us. Sometimes, however, we hold back on listening to Him. The best way to encounter this is simply to spend regular time with Him.

Invest your time, resources, energy, and conversations. Give everything that you can to Him, and He will bless you with a greater understanding of Him.

(Leader: Answer the following question first, and then encourage others to respond.)

What are spiritual markers and how are they significant in our spiritual maturity?

As the group responds, affirm their answers based on the content under "Spiritual Markers" (beginning on p. 82).

How did you note the spiritual markers in your life? What are some things God said to you as a teenager, college student, or young adult? (See page 84.)

What opened or closed doors are you presently facing?

How might God use your life for His kingdom through your career choices?

How is God using you where you are right now for His glory?

CLOSING

What did God say to you during the session today?

What will you do as a result?

Close in prayer and dismiss.

RELATIONSHIPS: FOR BETTER OR FOR WORSE

This session is based almost entirely on our interactions with others. Relationships of all kinds will be discussed. Be mindful that some in your group may have wounds not yet healed, so be sensitive with specific topics that may be still affecting group members negatively.

OPENING

Welcome the group and follow up on prayer requests mentioned during the previous session. Then invite the group to begin answering the review questions in small groups.

What information from the book has impacted you most? Why?

Of the five types of relationships mentioned this week, for which did you most need guidance? Why?

Call on volunteers to describe the worst and best relationships they have experienced in their lives.

What made the difference between the best and the worst?

Lead in prayer, asking God for leadership as you focus on relationships.

DISCUSSION

Friendships

Read John 13:1-20; then lead the group to answer the questions from page 96.

At what point in Jesus' life did He teach this lesson? Why was this time significant?

What lesson was Jesus trying to teach His disciples?

Why do you think Jesus concluded by saying, "whoever accepts me accepts the one who sent me"?

What are the characteristics of a good friend? (Refer to "Qualities of a Christian Friend," p. 98.)

Based on your evaluation of your own friendship qualities on pages 98–99, what changes did you identify that you need to make in the way you respond to others?

How does your love for others compare with Jesus' love for others?

Make a list of people who have impacted your life. What did these people do or say that positively influenced you?

Call on a volunteer to read Proverbs 27:17.

Lead the group to suggest ways this verse can be applied to relationships. Challenge them to form accountability partnerships with two or three others. Refer them to page 100 for ideas about accountability groups.

What do you consider to be the greatest dangers people face when approaching dating?

Review the five guidelines that will help single young adults maintain dating relationships that honor God and their dates (pp. 102–7).

If you're single, with which of these guidelines do you struggle the most?

Write the words *purity* and *temptation* on the board or a large sheet of paper. Lead the group to share their strategies for maintaining purity and avoiding temptation. Remind them of 1 Corinthians 10:13. Lead them to share their answers to the questions from page 107:

What does this verse say about temptation?

How does God deliver you from temptation?

How might this be applied to sexual temptation?

Divide the group into twos, pairing same-gender singles and same-gender marrieds. Instruct them to discuss the questions applicable to their life situation.

For Singles
What worries you most about marriage?

If you're in a dating relationship, how did you arrive at that point? How much time did it take? How much effort? How much sacrifice?

What criteria must your significant other meet in order to continue your relationship? What must he or she do for you to consider marriage?

For Marrieds
How much time and effort went into your relationship before you decided to marry? What sacrifices did you have to make to become one?

Return everyone to the large group.

What's the purpose of marriage?

Marriage is something that God entrusts to two Christ-seeking people who are willing to commit. It's a physical representation of Christ's love for us—an earthly example of Christ and His church.

What constitutes a proper marriage?

Why do almost half of all marriages end in divorce? What can stop Christian marriages from ending at such an alarming rate?

Society has lost the true meaning behind what a marriage is supposed to be about.

After a few minutes of discussion, review the three principles mentioned on pages 110–11. Call on volunteers to answer the following question from page 112:

What character traits does God require for those couples He uses and blesses?

How can you develop these traits in your dating or married relationships?

Families of Origin
Take a moment to share how your family has impacted your life. Call on volunteers to share the best qualities of their families.

Are you honoring your heritage? How?

What is God commanding you to do in Exodus 20:12? How do you do that?

What does honoring your father and mother look like at your age?

Why does God want us to obey and honor our families, even if they're not Christian role models?

How did the four principles for responding to hurtful parents (pp. 115–16) help you?

What actions have you taken this week to apply these principles?

If you have children, how can you instill in them obedience and honor? How does having children change your view of respecting your own parents?

What's one way you can honor your family (parents, siblings, and/or children) this week?

(Leader, answer the following question first to encourage other group members to respond.)

If you feel comfortable, tell if you've experienced a rocky place with a friend or family member. How did you respond? How does this situation affect the biblical call to honor your parents?

Relationships take a lot of work, time, patience, and a passion for people that only Christ can give us.

CLOSING ACTIVITY
Get with a partner, and if it's not too personal, talk about the steps you're going to take to mend or improve a specific relationship. Encourage partners to pray with each other when they finish conversation.

Pray for the relationships mentioned throughout the session, and then dismiss.

SESSION 5

CRISES: YOUR MOMENTS OF DECISION

OPENING

Welcome the group and follow up on prayer requests mentioned during the previous session. Then invite the group to begin a discussion of how to face crises.

Describe a crisis in the world that you have seen or heard about recently. How did hearing this news affect you?

What's the worst crisis you've ever experienced?

Read the following quotation: "A crisis is a challenge but also an opportunity for the Christian" (p. 125). (Leader, take a moment to answer the following question before asking your group.)

What did God teach you through a crisis you've experienced?

Lead the group in prayer, asking God for leadership as you examine how He uses crises in our lives to shape us and teach us.

DISCUSSION

None of us are immune to crisis in our lives.

Do you agree or disagree with this statement. Explain.

Enlist two people to read 2 Timothy 3:12 and Philippians 2:5-11.

What do these Scriptures teach us are the costs of following Jesus?

Do you think most Christians act as if being a Christian makes them less susceptible to crises in life or do they expect difficulties? Explain.

Lead the group to discuss their answers to the three questions on the top of pages 127–28:

Have you ever tried to be obedient to God, only to face hardships? What happened?

What good did God bring out of the challenges you faced? Did you allow God to work in His timing or take matters into your own hands? Explain.

Should Christians have to face hardships? Why or why not?

What promises has God given us regarding suffering? What are four reasons we can trust God through crises? (See "Four Reasons to Trust God," p. 130.)

Write the following on the board or a large sheet of paper: "Crises promote gaining life by losing it." Lead the group to discuss this apparent paradox. Challenge them to express circumstances in their lives that give evidence of this biblical truth.

Enlist someone to read John 12:24-25.

Discuss the following three questions from pages 131–32:

How do you save your life?

How do you lose your life?

How did Jesus illustrate this principle?

How does obeying God bring crises in our lives? What's the promise God has given us?

Even when facing overwhelming crises, we can trust that God will never leave us. Note the examples of Shadrach, Meshach, and Abednego.

What other people in the Bible faced crises because of their obedience? How did obedience cost Jesus?

Read Luke 8:22-25.

How does our response to moments of crises test our faith?

Explain that the word *sincere* comes from a term used in the ancient procedure of testing precious metals. Placed under extreme heat, trained merchants could determine whether a metal was pure or contained alloy. If the metal contained no alloy, it was determined to be *sincerus*, thus the origin of our English word *sincere*.

How is this ancient process of testing the sincerity of precious metals similar to the suffering that Christians endure?

Read Philippians 3:10.

What does it mean to share in the sufferings of Jesus? What does that mean you might have to sacrifice?

What is a God-sized assignment? How does God prepare you for one?

Read Matthew 26:36-46; Hebrews 5:7-10. Guide the group to discuss their answers to the three questions following "Jesus' Example" on page 151.

How does the way you handle crises compare with the way Jesus dealt with them?

Do you have friends, as Jesus did, to watch with you while you carry your heavy load? If so, how can you encourage them today? If not, what can you do to find such friends?

What do you need to turn over to God right now? Write a prayer to God giving all your concerns and difficulties to Him right now.

Arrange students in pairs and instruct them to discuss their answers to the top two questions from page 150:

When have you experienced a dark time? How were you able to overcome it?

How does God bring light to your difficult times?

Also discuss answers to the final two questions from page 151:

What did God say to you during the session today?

What will you do as a result?

Close in prayer for strength and faith to face the difficult circumstances mentioned today, and then dismiss.

CREATED FOR INTERDEPENDENCE: LIVING WITH GOD'S PEOPLE

OPENING

Write the following review questions on the board or on sheets of paper to distribute.

What's the chief cause of loneliness?

What's God's remedy?

Define the word *koinonia*.

As the group arrives, invite them to complete the quiz. Once everyone has had time to finish, call on volunteers to describe times of loneliness they've experienced.

What causes loneliness? How can we feel lonely even when we're not alone?

Lead in a time of prayer.

DISCUSSION

Arrange the group in threes and instruct them to discuss the following questions:

Would other people consider you interdependent or independent? Why?

How do you tend to be independent? How do you demonstrate interdependence?

Review this passage from page 156: "Sin affirms self and independence, leading to isolation and heartache. But God affirms interdependence, giving and receiving love and forgiveness. These lead to our fulfillment, interrelatedness, and mutual significance. Among the people of God you don't lose your identity, as secular critics will try to tell you, but rather it's in the group that your true identity is realized."

Read 1 Peter 2:9-10 and call on volunteers to share their answers to the questions regarding this passage:

What terms does this Scripture use to describe the people of God?

In what ways are they different than before?

Use information under "God's Remedy" (p. 156) to supplement the discussion.

What are some ways you can be a vital part of God's church now?

Lead students to brainstorm various ways the church is like a human body.

Would you consider yourself to be a dismembered part of the body of Christ or vitally attached? Explain.

Lead the group to discuss their answers to the following questions from page 162:

Read Ephesians 4:1-3,11-14 to see how Paul describes the church. Make a list of ways others build you up.

If you left town for a month, what ministries within your church would suffer?

How might God use you to build up—
teenagers?
families?
senior adults?
other young adults?

Discuss the three ways that young adults can effectively minister to one another: (1) helping one another, (2) forgiving one another, and (3) praying for one another. (See pp. 163–66.)

Call on a volunteer to explain the meaning of the Greek word *koinonia* (p. 168). After reading 1 John 1:3, call on people to share their responses to the questions from pages 168–69:

What is the distinguishing mark of Christians?

With whom do Christians have fellowship?

Lead the group to list a few ministries that have impacted their lives.

How have these ministries helped you experience *koinonia*? How can these ministries be more effective in helping others experience *koinonia*?

The church is called the *body* of Christ. As such we should communicate with and know one another. Culturally we might be quite different, but spiritually fellow church members are our brothers and sisters in Christ.

How can you bridge this gap and grow closer to your fellow brothers and sisters in Christ?

Think about the people in the worship services you attend that you don't know well. What steps can you take to get to know them?

Read 1 Corinthians 12:26.

What stands out to you in these verses?

How does your church or small group help one another in times of suffering? How do you celebrate other people's successes? What could you do better?

What activities could you do to intentionally care for and help other believers?

Believers should not only know one another, but they should also know how to work together for the greater good.

We're called together as believers and are one body of Christ, so we should be active in one another's lives. We should spend time together and pool our resources to help other people. This is not something that's limited to church-going Christians.

When was the last time you personally committed to someone in need? How did what he or she gained from your assistance compare to what you gained?

When was the last time your church helped beyond its walls? How were you involved?

Invite the group to share how God is using them to be on mission with their church. Summarize "Our Mission" from pages 178–79.

Do you believe God wants to use your church to impact your community? If so, how?

What must you adjust in your life in order to be a part of God's redemptive plan for your church?

What kinds of activities could you plan that would be inviting to unbelievers?

This is a great way to invite non-Christians and broken Christians to a safe, fun environment. This shows that Christians aren't cold and judgmental but rather welcoming and inviting. These times together don't have to be "churchy." Use it simply to express God's love for people, and He will bless your efforts. Pray for these opportunities and pray during these opportunities.

Praying with others and for others is important to your walk with Christ.

When was the last time you prayed with someone or had someone pray with you? How did you feel afterward?

What's something for which Christians gather together and pray? When does this happen? How often should it take place?

CLOSING

Ask the group to evaluate their answers to the last questions, "What did God say to you during your study today?" and "What will you do as a result?" for each day. Direct them to list their responses on a sheet of paper or index card. Challenge them to prayerfully consider immediate actions they need to take this week in response to what God is teaching them.

As you close, challenge the group to be on the lookout for an opportunity to serve. Pray and dismiss.

KINGDOM LIVING: GETTING THE BIGGER PICTURE

OPENING

Arrange the chairs in pairs or threes. As the group arrives, invite them to find a chair and to share with the person(s) seated near them at least one major takeaway from this study.

Call on a volunteer to read Matthew 6:33. Enlist a volunteer to lead in prayer, seeking God's wisdom and courage to obey this Word from Christ.

DISCUSSION

Summarize the BeachReach story on page 183.

What are some of the barriers that were overcome in this ministry? Do you think it's always worth the personal sacrifice involved to perform ministries like BeachReach? Why or why not?

We learned in day 1 that Jesus taught that becoming a citizen of the kingdom is the most important thing you'll ever do.

How would you support such a truth to someone who wanted to live for themselves and by the standards set by the world?

Direct students to find a partner and discuss their responses to the questions from page 189:

Do you find comfort in the fact that God will be absolutely just in His judgment of you? Explain.

How are you living your life as a kingdom citizen?

Ask for volunteers to share their answers to the questions from page 190:

What evidence in your life demonstrates that you are a child of the King?

What did God say to you during your study today?

What will you do as a result?

Explain the symbolism Jesus used to describe a Christian's part in God's kingdom. (See p. 192.)

What promises has God given us as partners in His kingdom?

Arrange the group into three teams and give each team one of the following assignments:

Team 1

A college student is faced with the dilemma of regularly attending a week-night Bible study or hanging out with his fraternity brothers. As a citizen of God's kingdom, how does he make the right decision?

Team 2

A young woman is faced with the dilemma of giving to her church's missions offering or buying Christmas gifts for her friends. As a citizen of God's kingdom, how does she make the right decision?

Team 3

A young man is faced with the dilemma of spending time alone with God in prayer and Bible study every day while struggling with accomplishing tasks for his full-time career. As a citizen of God's kingdom, how does this young man make the right decision?

After a few minutes, call the teams together to discuss their case studies.

Call on a volunteer to explain what's meant by the term *world Christian* on page 204. Refer the group to the evaluation they performed of their own lives as a world Christian on pages 203–4. Call on volunteers to share the changes they are making in order to be more involved in missions.

Read 2 Corinthians 5:9-10.

What was the major motivating factor affecting Paul's life? What does it mean to be accountable to God?

Read 1 Corinthians 3:13-15 and direct the group to share their responses to the questions from pages 207–8:

What will happen to the things you invest in during your life?

Is it possible to do nothing of eternal value and still enter heaven? How?

What kind of works will last in heaven?

CLOSING

Direct the group to choose partners and prayerfully discuss the questions under "Conclusion" on pages 209–10.

Share with the group other Bible study opportunities and ministry actions that will move them beyond this study to continued growth and ministry.

Explain: What you've completed in this seven-week study may actually be a beginning. Imagine this as the beginning of an exciting journey with Christ.

What will the following days look like?

Close in a prayer of thanksgiving and then dismiss.

MORE BIBLE STUDIES

ENGAGE
A PRACTICAL GUIDE TO EVANGELISM
BY J. D. GREEAR, ROB TURNER, DERWIN GRAY, AND BEN REED

The simple truth of the gospel doesn't change. And while this truth is timeless, we must always evaluate the presentation of that truth to make sure it's connecting in a culturally relevant way. This practical study examines the act of sharing your faith. It answers questions like, How do you begin a conversation about Jesus? What if people have questions you're not sure how to answer? What do you say if they respond positively or if they reject God's message?

MENTOR
HOW ALONG-THE-WAY DISCIPLESHIP WILL CHANGE YOUR LIFE
BY CHUCK LAWLESS

Drawing from biblical examples like Jesus and His disciples, Paul, and Timothy, author Chuck Lawless explores the life-transforming process of a mentoring relationship. This study is both a practical and a spiritual guide to biblical mentoring, providing easy-to-model life application for how to have and be a mentor.

ORDINARY
HOW TO TURN THE WORLD UPSIDE DOWN
BY TONY MERIDA

The kingdom of God isn't coming with light shows and shock and awe, but with lowly acts of service performed during the normal rhythms of life. *Ordinary* encourages participants to move into a life of mission and justice—speaking up for the voiceless, caring for the single mom, restoring the broken, bearing burdens, welcoming the functionally fatherless, and speaking the good news to people on a regular basis in order to change the world..

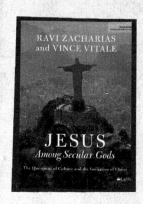

JESUS AMONG SECULAR GODS
THE QUESTIONS OF CULTURE AND THE INVITATION OF CHRIST
BY RAVI ZACHARIAS AND VINCE VITALE

As belief in the secular gods of atheism, hedonism, relativism, and humanism continues to grow, it's more important than ever for believers to be able to defend the claims of Christ. This Bible study challenges the popular and trending philosophies of the day, skillfully pointing out the fallacies in their claims and presenting compelling evidence for absolute truth as found in Jesus and as revealed in Scripture. Learn how to share your faith in a culture of opposing worldviews and articulate why you believe Jesus stands tall above all other gods.

LifeWay.com
800-458-2772
LifeWay Christian Stores